THE ART OF HELPING PEOPLE
OUT OF TROUBLE

THE ART
OF HELPING PEOPLE
OUT OF TROUBLE

BY
KARL DE SCHWEINITZ

BOSTON AND NEW YORK
HOUGHTON MIFFLIN COMPANY
The Riverside Press Cambridge

The Riverside Press
CAMBRIDGE · MASSACHUSETTS
PRINTED IN THE U.S.A.

TO
JESSIE DE SCHWEINITZ

Here in the maturity of print is the companion of our evenings and our holidays. How much a part of the household it has been! When the manuscript went to the publisher, you said that it was like having a child leave home, and in the book that has come back to us we shall see even more than the familiar features of a member of the family. We shall find a remembrance of shared experience and of being together, of cherished intimacies and a common enterprise, a keepsake of all that life has been, a pledge of all that we would have it be.

CONTENTS

INTRODUCTION   ix

I. THE ART OF LIVING   1

II. THE ART OF HELPING   21

III. WHEN TO HELP   33

IV. WHAT ONE MUST KNOW   41

V. SELF-REVELATION   58

VI. THE SOURCES OF UNDERSTANDING   77

VII. FACING THE FACTS   90

VIII. INTERPRETATION   105

IX. MEDIATION   121

X. PLANNING   139

XI. THE CULTIVATION OF RESPONSIBILITY   156

XII. MOTIVATION   179

XIII. DYNAMICS   203

XIV. IN CONCLUSION   224

INTRODUCTION

THE purpose of this book is to describe a method of helping people out of trouble. The principles underlying this method are applicable, not only when one is with an individual whose personal affairs are at a crisis, but whenever one finds himself so placed that he may influence other people — whether as parent, teacher, employer, or neighbor, whether with patient, parishioner, friend, or client.

It is a method both old and new, old in that its point of view toward life and many of its processes has been appreciated and used by understanding men and women since human beings first began to live and work together, new in that not until recent years has a sustained and directed effort to cultivate it been made.

This effort is being carried on by social workers and is inspired by their experience in meeting the perplexities and difficulties of the people who seek their help in clinics and hospitals, in schools and courts, in children's and family welfare or charity organization societies, and in many other institutions.

The method that has thus been developed has come to be known as social case work. The practice of it as applied to the more complicated forms of trouble is a vocation requiring, in addition to native ability, special knowledge and much preparation and training. There are many situations, however, in which this method may be of help to any one who can sympathetically interpret its spirit and its principles. Social case workers, having found it effective in the lives of those whom they serve and in their own lives also, believe that its point of view should form part of the philosophy of everybody and that an understanding of its processes would be useful in the daily relationships of life and particularly to those persons to whom other people turn for advice and guidance. It is in the interest of a wider application of social case work that this book has been written.

Social case work is not a panacea. While it can be helpful to any one in any economic or social status, it is not a cure of economic and social evils. Although an interpretation of it as universally applicable obviously avoids emphasis upon any one group of people, it must be remembered that where economic and social conditions are adverse, as they are for thousands of human beings, all the problems of life are aggravated, trouble is induced where trouble might otherwise be avoided, and its treatment is rendered vastly more difficult. The present discussion holds it to be axiomatic that only as environment and the organization of society improve can men and women hope to reach their fullest self-expression.

In illustrating the principles of social case work, I have made frequent use of incidents and crises that have arisen in human lives. Names and other identifying details have been changed. I hope that these stories will not lead the reader to think that the helping of people out of trouble is an instant and easy process. It is difficult, a matter usually of months and years, with many failures. Even some of the experiences which here appear to be successes were later followed by disaster, for just as a man may recover from one disease only to succumb to another, so, too, an individual, after overcoming one difficulty, may be overwhelmed by the next, or, as not infrequently happens, he may suffer from nervous and mental instabilities that prevent any permanent solution of his problems. Again and again the person who helps, and the person who is helped, struggle through mistake after mistake to achieve but a modicum of what they had hoped. Yet, despite all this there are successes, successes that more than justify faith in social case work as a method of helping people out of trouble, and as a key to the secret of a happier association with our fellows.

In the preparation of this book I have been helped by many persons, but particularly by my associates in the Family Society of Philadelphia.[1] Their insight and understanding, their experience and their skill are the inspiration of much that appears in the pages which follow.

[1] Formerly the Philadelphia Society for Organizing Charity.

THE ART OF HELPING PEOPLE
OUT OF TROUBLE

THE ART OF HELPING
PEOPLE OUT OF TROUBLE

.·.

CHAPTER I

THE ART OF LIVING

My cook wears a smiling, healthy, rather pleasing face. He is a
good-looking young man.... One day I looked through a little
hole in the shoji, and saw him alone. The face was not the same
face. It was thin and drawn and showed queer lines worn by old
hardship.... I went in, and the man was all changed — young
and happy again.... He wears the mask of happiness as an etiquette. (*The Japanese Letters of Lafcadio Hearn.*)

LIVING has yet to be generally recognized as one
of the arts. Being born and growing up are such
common experiences that people seldom consider
what they involve. As most readers of books pass
from cover to cover, realizing not at all that the
letters which form the words are the product of
painstaking craftsmanship and that the imposi-
tion of the type upon the page, the composition of
the title-piece, the binding of the volume, are the
result of centuries of study and design, so also we
take as a matter of course the miracle of being
alive, and the comings and goings of the men and
women about us.

No matter how close our neighbors, no matter how intimate our friends, we rarely appreciate the effort by which they achieve a mastery of life. This is a thing that they keep to themselves. Except in such moments of self-revelation as that in which Lafcadio Hearn found his Japanese cook, human beings truly wear the mask of happiness as an etiquette; since all the while they are engaged in a constant and relentless struggle.

For man is not born into a world made to fit him like a custom tailored suit of clothes, or a house built to order. He enters a universe that was eons old before his appearance, and that in all likelihood will continue for eons after his departure, an infinitely complex, eternally changing universe that evolves its processes unmindful of his presence. It sets the conditions. It is man who must do the fitting.

The task engrosses his every moment. He must adjust himself to the changeless laws of nature. He must adapt himself to the men and things about him. His very life at birth depends upon his ability in an instant to oxygenate his blood from the outside air instead of through the circulatory system of the mother. Within a very few hours he must learn the process of digestion.

As he grows older, he must accustom himself to variations in temperature, to the passage of the seasons, to the peculiarities of his physical environment. He must develop immunity from the swarm of bacterial parasites. Failure in many of these things may mean an end to his existence; yet they are the least perplexing adjustments he must make. For mostly they are automatic. In a sense they are beyond his conscious control. It is rather the adjustments to people and to events that involve the most vivid struggle. It is these which make the greatest demands upon his character and ability, and they throng every minute of every day.

His waking must be determined, not by the sun, but by the demands of his occupation. The time of breakfast and the food upon the table are the result of adjustment to the convenience and tastes of the different members of the household. His clothes must suit the weather and the day's engagements. He must adapt himself to train schedules, traffic regulations, library rules. He must compromise between his income and his needs and desires. Adaptations must be made to the house and to the neighborhood in which he lives, to manners and customs, to the organization of business, to the city, to the country, to accidents, to old age, to birth, to death.

Man is like a canoeist directing his course through waves. One after another he meets them. They may be heavy and powerful or they may be light ruffles of a sunshiny day in midsummer. He must ride them all. To each one he must slant his craft, dipping his paddle at just the right moment, giving it just the right twist, putting just the right amount of force into the stroke. Each wave requires a decision. Let him fail in judgment, or in skill and strength, and his canoe may ship water until it fills, or, in the lift of some great breaker, overturn immediately.

And as upon the ocean, a wave occasionally approaches which overtops its fellows, so, too, in life there towers before the voyager not infrequently a 'ninth born son of the hurricane and the tide.' These waves call forth all the skill that the mariner possesses. He who rides them may well count himself a master of the sea, for while the lesser adaptations of life cause many a wreck, it is these which occasion the greatest disasters. Would one learn to appreciate the art of living, he need but observe the manner in which people meet these portentous relationships and events.

Such are the adjustments to adolescence, to independence, to marriage, to single life, to widowhood, to a marked change in income, to sickness, to physical handicaps, to work, to parenthood, to disappointment in love, to the first visit away from home, to school, to college, to divorce, to home after the children have grown up and left it. Life is full of other similar situations. Not all of them are met by everybody, and people who have been confronted by the same problem find that to each individual it has presented itself in a different aspect. Yet one need study only a few of these experiences to realize that underlying all is the fundamental question of adjustment.

During adolescence there is the adjustment that accompanies the awakening of the child to the world outside the home. Hitherto the mother has been the refuge of sympathy and understanding, the father the source of recreation and adventure, and both the final authority upon questions of taste, of information, and of right and wrong. The boy — and in this he usually anticipates the experience of his sister — now discovers a kinship with those of his own age and develops an increasing respect for their standards of life and conduct. He becomes impatient of parental 'mays' and 'may nots,' all the more so because with the burgeoning of a new physique he is conscious of aspirations and emotions that he thinks the apparently staid and settled middle years cannot appreciate. He demands emancipation. He wants to be himself.

This spiritual emergence from the confines of the home does not often occur in a girl until she goes to work or to college. It then becomes a struggle for independence. Up to this time her goings and comings have been more closely supervised than those of her brother. In many households she is more her mother's daughter than she is herself. And now a greater freedom is opened to her. Going to work gives her the power of earned money and the broadened horizon of new companions. Going away to college brings her new associates and removes her from the immediate oversight of her parents. The result of either experience is to face her and her parents with much the same adjustment that her brother met in adolescence. The children seek self-expression and a larger control over themselves. The parents, regarding them still as children, want to continue to protect and direct them. Therein lies the possibility of conflict and the difficulty of the adjustment. If the parents draw the bonds of authority closer, if they place walls about the home, youth rebels, sometimes to yield to sullenness or to an irritable discontent, sometimes to break away from the life of the family altogether and to replace it with unstable and unsatisfactory friendships. If, however, mother and father recognize the right of the children to their own lives, the reason for conflict will disappear. Best of all is that attitude of the parents toward both daughter and son which fosters a gradual unfolding and increasing of the girl's and the boy's responsibility, so that this phase of the adjustment to adolescence and independence never becomes critical or even conscious, but takes place as part of the evolution from childhood to youth and from youth to adult life.

The adjustment to marriage involves an institution that, ever changing, is yet ever the same. It varies as human beings vary. In the homes of neighbors it may exist in the tradition of one hundred years ago and as a prophecy of what it may be to-morrow.

The twentieth century finds it a more democratic and a more spiritual relationship than ever it has been before. Man is now an integral part of the family in contrast to the days when he was lord and the woman subject. Then he was in a sense superior to the family and outside of its laws. For spiritual and intellectual companionship he looked to other men, and both before and in marriage, society condoned in him a standard of sex morality different from that which it demanded of his wife.

To-day, woman, with vastly increased opportunity for education and with an extension of interest to all human activities, offers to man a relationship that is rich in its intellectual and spiritual possibilities. She is capable of a fineness and delicacy of appreciation that challenges his understanding, while the single standard of sex morality causes the physical basis of marriage to be of increasing significance.

Even the appearance of the home has become a factor in determining the success of the association of husband and wife. The business of financing and administering the household calls forth ever greater ability and the growing appreciation of the psychology of childhood has added to the importance of the family as an educational institution.

Marriage is the most complicated of all adjustments, for the man and the woman must adapt themselves, not only to a new task and a new environment, but they must determine the form of that task and the character of that environment, and they must do this, not each for himself, but together. Two individualities, two sets of likes and dislikes, and of manners and mannerisms, two sexes, two products of different inheritance and experience, must combine to give expression to a new entity, the family. It is the most intimate of all relationships. In it there is no such thing as the impersonality which simplifies association with human beings in other situations. Always there is the intangible emotional factor, capable of thwarting every attempt at adjustment or of making easy the adaptation of personalities whose union would otherwise be impossible. Analyze it though one may, marriage will continue to escape definition. It will be discussed and debated through the coming generations as it has been through the past, and yet will ever hold the quality of mystery, offering to its votaries an enduring source of happiness.

As the adjustment to marriage is not accomplished in a day, but must be made as long as the man and the woman continue to be husband and wife, so also the adjustment to single life is a process of years. With a woman it begins usually midway between twenty and thirty. She is then mature, but not so settled that adjustment to another personality would be difficult. She is physically best equipped for the bearing of children. She has completed her formal education. If she has been at work, she has served her apprenticeship. All that has gone before has been a preparation. Nature and custom define marriage and motherhood as the next step. But the same intangible factor which can make or mar marriage cuts across her path. She does not meet the man with whom she would mate.

This is not a decision that can be made finally. The possibility of marriage affects her plans for ten or fifteen years, or even longer. If, as now most single women do, she turns toward a career, she is not likely to make the same whole-hearted adjustment to it as that of which a man is capable. Uncertainty about the future renders it difficult for her to be constant in work.

Unless she finds opportunity for achievement in civic activities, or in business, she may develop a feeling of ineffectiveness because of what she may consider to be her failure to marry. She may think that there is a questioning in the minds of her friends, and in so thinking she may become supersensitive in her relations with other people.

Far more serious and more difficult of adjustment than either the feeling of uncertainty or that of ineffectiveness is the lack of an emotional outlet. That part of the single woman's nature which in marriage would be directed toward lover, husband, and child has not this trinity of the affections. In its place she must find a medium for expression. The quality of her relationship with her parents and the other members of the family becomes therefore of greater importance to her than to her married sister. This is true of all her friendships, particularly of her friendships with women. As she grows older, she probably finds her association with men increasingly casual and infrequent. She must replace this with other interests, taking care to avoid the dangers of an ingrowing existence that expresses itself in a frigidity in personal relationships or in a parasitic emotion for some other woman.

To chart a straight course through the shoals and reefs of single life, to attain to the happiness of dignified and affectionate friendships, to keep a sense of proportion and balance, to maintain a tolerance of temperament and attitude is truly an achievement. Yet women are making this adjustment, developing in the process richer personalities, and sounding new depths of understanding and appreciation.

The single man usually is close to thirty years before his thoughts are affected by the fact that he is not married. With him marriage is not a career as with woman. It is rather a motive for a career. Lacking this, he must combat a feeling of futility. He has no one for whom to labor. The tendency in the single woman toward instability in work becomes with him an instability in his manner of living. He has no sense of permanence in abode or in his social relations. Helping still further to unsettle him is the solicitude of his friends. He is never allowed to forget that he ought to be married. There is always the implication of a responsibility shirked.

The instinct to parenthood is generally not so dynamic a force in him as in woman. It rarely develops until after he becomes a father, but there is a compensating instinct to protect. Frequently this transfers itself into loyalty and devotion to his mother, who may, particularly if she is a widow, consciously or unconsciously, play upon this instinct, preventing both his marriage and the free development of his career.

In making the adjustment to single life, the man must guard both against a devotion of this kind which hinders him from attaining to a true self-expression, and against a self-centered existence that at the worst may drift into sensuality. At the best he may, in adjusting himself to single life, achieve an intense application to work and a variety of interests and friendships that can bring him a large measure of happiness.

Widowhood, like all other adjustments, presents itself under a multitude of varying circumstances. The widowhood which follows a happy marriage is primarily the adjustment to a great loneliness, a loneliness that is both spiritual and physical. Life has hitherto been arranged on a communal basis; the family instead of the individual has been the unit, every responsibility has been shared, the habit of intimate association with another person has been formed. Now this is all changed. Some people attempt to fill the empty place by summoning memories of the past and idealizing the one who has gone, a form of substitution which if indulged too greatly may degenerate into self-pity and a withdrawal from wholesome activity. Far wiser is it to rely upon work and other interests, inside the home or without, in which variety and inspiration can play their part.

Children both simplify and complicate the adjustment. They provide an outlet for the affections, but they offer the temptation to emotional dependence. Some parents become almost parasitic in this respect, handicapping the children in their efforts at self-expression and preventing them from the freedom which their development requires. Even where this does not happen, the problem of training and of education is most difficult. The mother must be both father and mother. Hitherto, the children have had the benefit of the thought and experience of two people. Widowhood involves a loss which the mother cannot make up by duplicating herself through the devotion of more time and energy. She must seek other contacts and other associates for her children to compensate them for what their father would have contributed.

When it is the father who has been left, the problem becomes still more perplexing. Only too often in the absence of the mother the family breaks. She has been the home, and without her the whole structure collapses, leaving the husband to make a new adjustment to single life, and the children to face the whole series of difficulties which confronts those who are homeless and orphaned.

Sickness involves a twofold adjustment, the adjustment which the patient must make to his disease and that which his family and his friends must make to him. In either case the crux of the problem is much the same. What is he able to do and what is he unable to do? What exertion is wise and what is not wise? When should he yield to invalidism and when should he refuse to listen to the suggestion of ill-health? When should he reconcile himself to a continuance of nursing and when should he resume activity? When should his friends take care of him and when should they expect him to take care of himself? It is a problem that the diagnosis of the physician cannot always solve, for it has as much to do with the spirit as with the body. Often, the commiseration of friends and their desire to pamper is a more insidious foe for the patient to overcome than the bacteria of his disease.

Sometimes sickness affects the attitude and expression of the invalid so that he becomes a different person from what he would wish to be. Then all that experience, insight, and understanding can provide are required by his friends so that they can appreciate the reasons for his otherwise inexplicable behavior, and make the necessary allowances for it. This is particularly true when the man is not confined to his bed, but is suffering one of the minor and less apparent chronic illnesses. Wherever sickness appears, it brings new and unforeseen problems. There are few things that more quickly precipitate the true character of an individual and his friends.

Work is one of the most important of adjustments because it is chief among the mediums through which a man expresses his personality. Let Colas Breugnon describe it:

"There is one old chum that never goes back on me, my other self, my friend — my work. How good it is to stand before the bench with a tool in my hand and then saw and cut, plane, shave, carve, put in a peg, file, twist and turn the strong fine stuff, which resists yet yields — soft smooth walnut, as soft to my fingers as fairy flesh; the rosy bodies or brown limbs of our wood-nymphs which the hatchet has stripped of their robe. There is no pleasure like the accurate hand, the clever big fingers which can turn out the most fragile works of art, no pleasure like the thought which rules over the forces of the world, and writes the ordered caprices of its rich imagination on wood, iron, and stone. . . . To serve my art the elves of the sap push out the fair limbs of the trees, lengthen and fatten them until they are polished fit for my caresses. My hands are docile workmen, directed by their foreman, my old brain here, and he plays the game as I like it, for is he not my servant too? Was ever man better served than I?"

Here was a well-adjusted workman. He had what every one needs: an employment in which his faculties had the freest possible play. Happy is that person who finds this in his pursuit of a livelihood. A man cannot expend too great pains in the search for appropriate employment. Sometimes it is a quest of years, involving many trials. The more encouragement, therefore, should we offer the youth who, after leaving school or college, experiments with a number of different occupations. Instead of being reminded of the dismal proverb about the rolling stone, he should be received with sympathy and with interest and should be helped to discover the best channel for self-expression and service.

Sometimes this means creating in his present employment the desired opportunity. Imagination and invention can often delve into their own environment and find the seeds of growth. There are, however, many jobs that are so mechanical, so limited in scope, and so monotonous in the activities which they require, that there is little hope for self-expression in them. Those who earn their living in such ways, if they cannot change their work, should seek place for the play of their faculties in an avocation. There are many examples of this. Hawthorne's interest was writing, but he supported himself for years by a clerkship in a customs house. A man may be an operative in a factory and yet may make the art of photography his work, and not infrequently an inspired evangelist is concealed within the overalls of a janitor or behind the leathern apron of a cobbler.

Self-expression in work includes more than the achievement of brain and hand. It is dependent also upon the quality of the association that the individual has with his fellows. The office and the shop stand next to the home in the adaptability that they require of people. They are the very crossroads of life where personalities meet and pass and where there are multitudes of human contacts.

Truly the adjustment to work is enough alone to call forth all the skill that a man possesses. What renders it and every other adjustment vastly more difficult is the presence at the same time of other problems. It is not possible for him to concentrate upon work to the exclusion of everything else; for while he is making this adaptation he may also be confronted with the adjustment to illness or with the necessity of helping his son to meet the problems of adolescence. The adjustment to widowhood may be accompanied by a sudden change in income. The adaptations to single life and to unemployment may appear together. The adjustment to marriage may include the adjustment to parenthood.

Rarely do adjustments come alone and rarely do they concern only one person. Usually a number of people are affected. In marriage, man and woman and the relatives of both may be involved: in independence, the woman and her family; in work, employer and employee; in sickness, the invalid and the household.

The problem is always complex, and it is universal. All about us the struggle is going on, and in it human beings everywhere are engaged; silently, perhaps, and with countenances as cheerful as that of Lafcadio Hearn's Japanese cook, but none the less intently. Event succeeds event; accidents, people, happenings, one after another come toward us. Each must be met and dealt with, and upon the manner of our dealing depends the issue of our lives. If successful, men say that we are happy. If unsuccessful, they say we are in trouble. For this process of adjustment is life, and the mastery of it is the art of living which, who that considers the stakes, will deny to be the greatest of all the arts.

CHAPTER II

THE ART OF HELPING

Behavior — fresh, native, copious, each one for himself or
    herself,
Nature and the Soul expressed — America and freedom ex
    pressed — In it the finest art,
In it pride, cleanliness, sympathy, to have their chance,
In it physique, intellect, faith — in it just as much as to manage
    an army or a city, or to write a book — perhaps more,
The youth, the laboring person, the poor person, rivalling all
    the rest — perhaps outdoing the rest,
The effects of the universe no greater than it;
For there is nothing in the whole universe that can be more effec-
    tive than a man's or woman's daily behavior can be,
In any position, in any one of these States.

WALT WHITMAN

GREATEST of all the arts, living is also the most
exacting in its demands upon its practitioners. It
delights in crises. It chooses its own times and
seasons, considering neither the convenience nor
the preparedness of its followers. It may present
itself in some instant dilemma or it may develop
its problems so gradually that one does not realize
that an adjustment is at hand. It appears char-
acteristically in the sort of cumulative sequences
that seem to pile difficulty upon difficulty, giving
rise to the saying that troubles never come singly.
Age, youth, wealth, experience — none of these

does it spare or respect. It compels the attention and the energy of all mankind.

It is the most exacting of the arts, but it is not beyond mastery. Men have achieved it, are achieving it constantly. Rare is he who has not a fundamental capacity to adjust himself to life. When a man fails where his neighbors succeed, when under substantially the same economic and physical conditions and in the same crisis he falls into trouble which they avoid, it is not necessarily because he lacks the ability to achieve. It may be because he is prevented from using the powers with which he has been endowed. He is blocked; he is handicapped; he is not free. He is bound by habits, emotions, fears, prejudices, superstitions. He is thwarted by those with whom he is intimately associated in work or in pleasure, even by his friends, by the members of his family. He is thrust into trouble as was the little girl whose teacher said of her:

"If Martha is learning anything I don't know it. She never answers any questions. She never has anything to say in class. She just sits and looks."

So stupid did Martha appear to be that until an examination at a psychological clinic showed that she was of sound mind, it was thought that she might possibly be feeble-minded. The difficulty had its chief cause in the behavior of the child's mother.

Martha's parents had wanted their first born to be a boy. That the baby should have been a girl was a great disappointment, and when a son came as their next child, Martha was thrust into the second place. Harry was given precedence in everything. Reproach was always her portion. She was continually being compared with her brother to her own disadvantage.

She would hear her mother tell visitors:

"Martha is stupid, but Harry is bright. Why, Harry even has to help Martha with her lessons."

If it was suggested that Martha run an errand, her mother would say:

"Oh, Martha can't do that. I'll have Harry do it."

When an operation to remove adenoids was prescribed for Martha, her mother exclaimed in her presence:

"Martha will never go to the hospital. She'll just cry. I'll never get her to go."

On another occasion the child was obliged to listen to this comment upon her character:

"When Martha gets a nickel, she keeps it to herself. Harry buys candy and gives it to the other children. But not Martha. You wouldn't catch her giving anything away. She's sort of sly."

Is it surprising that Martha should have been silent in school? Ever since she had been able to remember, her every effort at self-expression had been discouraged before it had had so much as a chance to start. Daily she was being told that she was an inferior person, that she was capable of nothing, and that she amounted to nothing. She was bound as effectively as if she had been in chains. She was shut up within herself by the very person who should have fostered her development. She was not free to adjust herself to life.

Only after the mother had been shown the part she was playing in her daughter's unhappiness did the child begin to receive the opportunities she needed. A changed atmosphere at home and special attention in school released her from her handicaps and stimulated her in the use of her abilities. Not many months had passed before the mother herself said:

"There's the greatest difference in Martha. She's a changed girl."

It is seldom that trouble is so exclusively due to the limitations which people place around an individual. Usually it is brought about by a combination of restrictions from without and inhibitions within. This is illustrated by the difficulty which Stuart Weston found in making one of the most common adjustments, the adjustment to sickness.

His disease was tuberculosis. He had been ill for three years. Most people in such a predicament follow the advice of a physician and take the cure at a sanatorium. This Weston did not do. Despite the urging of his friends and his medical advisors, he remained at home, working intermittently, as his health permitted. Gradually he grew weaker. His family also suffered. At the end of three years his wife was showing the strain of having his invalidism added to the care of five boys and girls. Two of the children had developed symptoms suggestive of tuberculosis, and discouragement had settled down over the whole family.

The causes of this failure to make the adjustment to sickness lay partly with Weston and partly with the people and things about him. He had been prejudiced against the State Sanatorium by false reports of how its patients suffered from neglect. A young woman who had lived across the street from his home had gone there and died. Weston thought he might meet the same fate. He was afraid, also, that if he should go to the sanatorium, his mother-in-law would see to it that there would be no home awaiting him when he returned. He and his mother-in-law had never been able to endure each other. If he was self-sufficient, self-reliant, and self-assertive, so too was she, and at every point they clashed. Weston suspected — perhaps not wholly without justification — that she would use his absence to induce his wife to come and live with her. This meant to him that Mrs. Weston, who lacked the force to resist so strong a will, would become a drudge at the boarding-house which her mother conducted, that the children would be placed in institutions, and that the life of the family would be broken.

Along with this fear was Weston's feeling that he was being overlooked. His pride was hurt by the attitude from which he thought people now regarded him. In the years when all was well, he had been the head of the household. He had made the decisions and his will had dominated every plan. Now that he was sick, those who had come to help him failed to consult him about his family. Conversation with him was limited to efforts to persuade him to enter the sanatorium. Gradually he came to feel that he was regarded only a- something to be got rid of, a case to be sent away whether he wanted to go or not. His hurt feelings blocked his judgment. He was no longer free in thought or in action, and he remained at home.

The social worker who was asked to help recognized that here lay the heart of Weston's difficulty. She appreciated his desire to plan for himself and his family, and began at once to seek his advice at every step, bringing his wife into their discussions, so that his decisions were not solitary as they had been before his illness, but were made with Mrs. Weston participating. As soon as Weston realized that his opinion was being considered, and that he was once more a factor in the destinies of the household, he ceased to feel the pique which had been blocking his judgment. He could now think much more clearly about his disease and the appropriate treatment.

The fear that his mother-in-law would break up his home could be allayed only by assurances from the woman herself. These were procured by an appeal to her sympathies. Weston was explained to his mother-in-law. She was shown that the traits to which she objected were, after all, only the evidences of a strong character; that it was his very devotion to his family which kept him at home, and that his whole hope of recovery lay in his going away to the sanatorium in an easy frame of mind. The mother-in-law was persuaded at least to the point of neutrality, and, indeed, a little beyond, for she helped in the preparations for Weston's journey.

Meanwhile, Weston's prejudice against the State Sanatorium had been met by efforts to arrange for his admission to another institution. While the attempt was unsuccessful, it showed Weston that he was not being forced to go where he did not wish to go; and when it was suggested that in the absence of any other place he make a trial of the State Sanatorium, with the understanding that if he did not like it he should return, he went quite willingly. It is a long-established principle of human nature that to say "you must" when a man says "I won't" only makes his "no" the firmer, while to set him free to do as he pleases dissipates his opposition and releases his energies for a wise decision.

Even more difficult than the adjustment which

the sick person must make to his illness is that which is often involved for the other members of the household. Certainly, this was true of the problem with which Mrs. Slater was confronted. Following an attack of influenza, her husband had found it difficult to recover his strength. He could not summon his energies in the way that for the past few years had made him a valuable and trusted workman. He left a steady job and began wandering about the country. Sometimes he sent money to his family. Sometimes he did not. Sometimes he wrote home and sometimes he forgot to do so. Finally he consulted a physician who returned paresis as the diagnosis. The prognosis was a slow mental deterioration that would finally leave him wholly irresponsible.

Mrs. Slater could not accept this fact. She would not believe that her husband's illness was serious or that he was not a competent human being. She continued to expect him to be the person he had been and to play his usual part in the family life. When he failed to do so, she showed a resentment that occasionally expressed itself in a sharp and exacting attitude toward Mr. Slater as guilty of desertion and non-support, but more often in a bitterness toward other people and in a struggle for the rehabilitation of her husband that took her attention from home and children.

This failure to adjust herself to her husband's illness was chiefly due to her unwillingness to face the disappointment that the acceptance of it involved. Mrs. Slater came of an industrious, orderly, hard-working stock, thrifty, steady, home-abiding people to whom the unusual seldom happened. Mr. Slater was her great adventure. He swept into her life with a picturesqueness and a glibness that thrilled and fascinated her. His had been a vagabond youth, spent chiefly at the races where he knew the bookmakers as well as the horses. He was all that Mrs. Slater's family was not; careless about money, ready to trust everything to chance, and a most interesting person. Mrs. Slater sensed a certain dubiousness in the attitude of her relatives and became engaged without having confided her love affair to any one.

Within a year after her wedding, it became evident that she had married a dissipated fellow who was given to drunken sprees and who could not be depended upon to provide for himself and his family. Frequently during a period of six or seven years she was obliged to seek shelter with her parents for him and the children. She felt his failure keenly, and her pride forbade her the relief that she might have had by unburdening herself to her mother.

Then there came a great change in Mr. Slater. He awoke from one of his sprees to a sense of sin. He was converted from his old ways. He joined a rescue mission, and for four years he was a man to be pointed out as an example. This was the happiest time in Mrs. Slater's married life. She could now be proud of her husband. He was the successful head of his family, a steady workman, and a leader in the church. Her judgment in marrying him was vindicated.

It was this period of happiness that the development of paresis brought to a close. Mrs. Slater could not believe that it was the end. She had only just become accustomed to prosperity. She had participated vicariously in her husband's achievements. Her romance had come true. That it must all cease was too terrible to think about. She could not adjust herself to the new situation. She was too beclouded with emotion to face the facts.

Yet it was precisely this which she must do if she was to be of any use to herself or to her husband or to the children. The social case worker whom she consulted began a work of interpretation that continued for months. She prepared Mrs. Slater for the doctor's report that it was paresis, not influenza, which was affecting Mr. Slater. She explained the course which the disease might be expected to take and how it might affect his behavior. When Mrs. Slater insisted that the pain which her husband suffered after the use of salvarsan indicated that the doctors did not know anything about his trouble, the experiences of other people were cited as proof that this was the frequent consequence of these treatments. When Mr. Slater in a sudden flash of energy enjoyed a brief prosperity, the social worker kept in touch with Mrs. Slater so that she could prepare her for the ultimate collapse. Always what had been foretold about the disease took place, until Mrs. Slater began to perceive what was inevitable.

She had lost her husband. He could no longer be the source of interest and inspiration which, despite his weaknesses, he had always been to her; but there were the children, which in the struggle of the past months she had neglected. Here was a means of renewal and strength. Could she discover in the care of them an outlet for the energy which had been going into the vain attempt to prove that her husband was a normal man, she might achieve a measure, at least, of happiness. An opportunity was found for her to spend a day or two a week as a mother's helper in a family where she might observe what child training can mean. This gave her a new vision, while the fact that she was appreciated by her employer brought her assurance and confidence for the meeting of her own problems. Gradually the hope that she had built upon her husband's recovery was transferred to an interest in the education of her children and the making of her adjustment had been begun.

The principles involved in the solution of Mrs. Slater's problem were fundamentally the same as those underlying the treatment of the difficulties of Weston and of the little girl who was silent in school. Each one of these persons was blocked by fears and inhibitions of various kinds. They were stopped from the free use of their energies. They needed to be released from the cramping influence of unfavorable associates and of their own emotions. For the little girl this was accomplished by giving her greater opportunity for self-expression in school and by helping her mother to under stand her. For Weston it was done by sympathetically interpreting him to his mother-in-law and by enabling him to return to a larger self-determination both in the making of plans for the family and in the selection of the place in which he would try to overcome his disease. For Mrs. Slater it was achieved by assisting her to face the dreaded fact of her husband's mental condition, and by finding for her in the welfare of her children a new channel for activity.

The details of what was done for each of these persons varied, but the goal of the work was the same. Whatever processes are followed in helping a man out of trouble, whether or not they consist, as here, in interpreting people to each other and to themselves, in stimulating initiative and in opening opportunity for self-expression, they should all focus upon the task of releasing the individual from the misunderstandings, the inhibitions, and the restrictive influences that block his development, and of encouraging him always to a higher use of his abilities. To help a man in this way is to prepare him for the making of all his adjustments and to set him upon the road to the mastery of the art of living. Let life be ever so exacting, it yields itself to him who is free.

CHAPTER III

WHEN TO HELP

The principle of guidance cannot be separated from the thing guided. It recalls a parable of Charles Kingsley's which he related to Huxley. A heathen khan in Tartary was visited by a pair of proselytizing moollahs. The first moollah said, 'O Khan, worship my God. He is so wise that he made all things!' Moollah Number Two said, 'O Khan, worship my God. He is so wise that he makes all things make themselves.' Number Two won the day. (JOHN BURROUGHS, in "A Critical Glance into Darwin," *Atlantic Monthly*, August, 1920.)

THE first and the hardest lesson to learn about people who are in trouble is that they can be helped only if they want to be helped. There is no such thing as making an adjustment for somebody else. Only the husband and wife can make the adjustment to marriage; only the mother and father can make the adjustment to parenthood; only the widow to widowhood. No one can live another person's life. No one can overcome a single disadvantageous habit for him. No one can make him strong by working for him. No one can make him think by thinking for him. Whatever of happiness an individual achieves depends fundamentally upon himself. However great the opportunities that may be offered to him, however wise the suggestions that may be made to him, unless he himself is desirous of profiting by them, they can accomplish nothing for him.

What causes this lesson to be especially difficult to learn is the instinct to help that dwells in all of us, an instinct so powerful that often we cannot resist its impulses. Frequently it forces us to spend our energies in trying to help where help is untimely, where the individual is not ready to change, and where, therefore, he benefits not at all, or, at least, very little by what we do.

The only satisfactory approach to helping a person out of trouble is that which is made in response to a request for help. This need not be a formal request. It may be conveyed by a look or in a chance remark. Like the patient who seeks a physician for the relief of the symptoms of his disease rather than for the cure of the malady itself, the individual in difficulty may ask assistance in something incidental to the real problem. The girl whose difficulties with her family have culminated in her running away from home may inquire about a job, but a question or two will show her trouble to lie deeper. A man may seek a loan when actually his difficulty is a maladjustment to work.

The desire for help may be variously indicated.

but there must be at least some sign of dissatisfaction or some stirring of the urge to better things. Occasionally one will be placed in such a professional or friendly relationship that he can stimulate this desire, but usually, unless its presence is evidenced by an appeal for assistance, an attempt to give advice will start under unfavorable auspices and with little chance of success. Without such a request, how can we tell whether the person in trouble has any confidence in us and in our ability to be of service?

Often what we, looking at a life from without, may think is trouble may not be trouble at all, but only a different way of living from that which we prefer. Husband or wife out of a far more intimate knowledge than ours may be able to discount each for the other words or behavior that seem to us intolerable, while parents may have a far more healthy relation with their children when they are alone with them than when they are conscious of being observed. Or it may be that an individual may willingly endure handicaps in his personal life because other things are more important to him. That sometimes is the price of genius. It is frequently through the storm and the stress of unfulfilled emotion, through trouble and unhappiness, that the great achievements of art and science are attained. Until such an individual indicates that he wants advice, it is not for us to urge our services upon him.

There are, however, situations in which one is justified in intervention even against the will of the person in difficulty. These are when a man is demonstrably incapable of managing his own affairs, when he is so neglectful of his children as to endanger their morals and their physical well-being, or when he does this deliberately, and when he is a menace to the health and life of his associates. Society has recognized such conditions as prejudicial to its welfare and has established laws and a definite procedure for dealing with them when they arise. For the person who is of unsound mind, it is possible through the courts to have a guardian appointed, and, if necessary, to have the mentally defective individual committed to an institution. The court can take children from parents who are ill-treating or neglecting them, and in many States the department of health has authority to remove from his home the diseased person who is endangering the health of his family and of his neighbors. There is vast room for discussion about when a man is incapable of managing his own affairs and when he is a menace to the health and life and morals of others, but experience in bringing questions of this sort before the courts enables public health officials and social case workers to know what evidence will be required by judges and lawyers; and when a family appears to be suffering by reason of the actions of one or more of its members, it is wise to consult the appropriate municipal department or social agency before acting.

Except in situations of this sort, intervention that is not invited runs the risk of failure. This may mean having to watch a friend's distress grow greater and greater when we feel certain that we could be of assistance. Often, however, matters must become worse before they can become better. Sometimes a man must reach the depths before the realization of his misery becomes strong enough to imbue him with the will to achieve a solution of his problems.

There is always the hope that he may of his own strength be able to overcome his difficulties; and this is vastly more important than that we should have the satisfaction of aiding him. The sense of achievement and of power that springs from meeting and making his own adjustments is too precious a possession to be denied to any human being. That which makes for the development of the person in trouble, which increases his strength, which adds to his character, should be the goal of every one who truly cares for other people; and there is nothing which will do more to forward the winning of this goal than the solution of a man's problems by himself.

It is when he decides that this is not possible that the time for help comes. So long as he does not run counter to the lives of others, our service to him is greatest when we await his call for assistance; when we undertake the art of helping only after having been asked to help.

CHAPTER IV

WHAT ONE MUST KNOW

When you meet with a fact opposed to a prevailing theory, you should adhere to the fact and abandon the theory, even when the latter is supported by great authorities and generally adopted. (CLAUDE BERNARD, quoted by René Valléry Radot, in his *Life of Pasteur*.)

To help a man out of trouble one must know and understand him. This would seem to be axiomatic. The surgeon does not operate until he is intimately acquainted with the physical condition of his patient. The lawyer does not venture an opinion upon a contract without first informing himself about the legal issues involved. Before ever ground is broken, the architect has ascertained how much stress each floor of the projected building will bear. No one would entrust a watch to a jeweler who began by indiscriminately pottering among springs and pinions instead of intelligently endeavoring to discover what was wrong. Certainly, then, when the difficulty concerns a human being, we should approach its adjustment from as complete a knowledge and understanding of him as it is possible to obtain.

Yet knowledge and understanding are precisely

the elements most frequently lacking in human relationships. Although people have learned the value of the fact in science and in dealing with material things, they have still to make any general application of it in their association with each other. Here supposition usually has precedence over information. Prejudice outranks evidence and impulse comes before reason. There is no better proof of this than the number of voters, who, without so much as an attempt at verification, allow their electoral decisions to be influenced by the slanders which are whispered about the personal lives of political candidates. The world made up its mind about revolutionary Russia before it had learned to know either Russia or the revolution; and it is not only the schoolgirl, who, without inquiry into causes, pronounces as 'stuck up' the acquaintance who does not notice her as she passes by.

This failure to appreciate the importance of examination and understanding enters even into the family circle. It jeopardizes the harmony between husband and wife and makes difficult the bringing-up of children. Mark Twain's account of how Aunt Polly punished Tom Sawyer for breaking a sugar bowl, which he had not broken, is typical of what happens in many homes

One evening, it will be remembered, Aunt Polly caught Tom stealing sugar from the table and rapped his knuckles by way of reproof. Later, while she was out of the room, Sid, Tom's usually well-behaved half-brother, reached for the sugar bowl. It slipped between his fingers and fell to the floor. Aunt Polly returned and discovered the fragments. Tom awaited the punishment of the offender, not without a certain sense of satisfaction, but "the next instant he was sprawling on the floor! The potent palm was uplifted to strike again when Tom called out: 'Hold on, now, what er you belting me for? Sid broke it!'

"Aunt Polly paused perplexed." She had punished the wrong boy. Of course, she was too proud to confess her error, and, overcome with self-pity, Tom stalked away into the night. Life was awry between nephew and aunt. If only Aunt Polly had stopped to learn the facts!

She was, however, no different from the rest of human beings in this respect. One need not look far to find many repetitions of her mistake. There was Mrs. Brown whose relatives were estranged from her because of the constant crying of her baby. The family blamed the mother's lack of firmness. They said that the child cried because he had not been properly trained. He had all the appearance of health, and so it did not occur either to the mother or to the relatives that he might not be well. Finally, the situation became so uncomfortable for Mrs. Brown that she left her home. The difficulty was brought to the attention of a social case worker, who suggested that the baby be examined by a physician. A slight intestinal trouble was discovered which an operation corrected. The boy ceased his fretfulness and the cause of difference between the mother and the relatives was removed.

Social case work abounds in similar illustrations, showing how dependent upon facts human problems are for their solution. It is seldom possible to recognize at sight the nature of another person's trouble. Usually what we see on first acquaintance are only symptoms. People generally postpone seeking advice about their personal affairs until they are facing a crisis, and then it is their immediate perplexity from which they want relief. It bulks so large that often they can think of nothing else and emphasize it to the exclusion of the real problem. So it is that one of the first lessons to be learned about helping other people is the importance of looking behind the present difficulty for the disturbing cause, of diagnosing the adjustment that must be made.

It is essential, also, to discover the things within and without the individual to which he can turn for the material he may need in building his life anew. This involves learning to know the personal characteristics of the man who is in trouble: his appearance, his mannerisms, his disposition and temperament, his qualities of character, his habits and his interests, his ambitions, his desires, his talents, his skills, his physical and mental capacity.

It involves learning whether he has any plan for meeting his difficulties and what that plan is, and how he has met similar problems in the past. Likewise is it important to be acquainted with the extent and variety of his resources. What are his assets? They may be many and varied. When a man is suddenly stricken with illness, his most valuable resource may be the hospital that his taxes or his contributions have been instrumental in maintaining. Membership in a civic club was one of the assets which a woman used in making her adjustment to widowhood. When her husband died, she found in her efforts to improve living conditions in her neighborhood an interest that helped to fill the gap that death had made in her life.

To be informed about a man's savings and his credit, or their absence, may be as important in aiding him to solve his problems as information of this kind would be in reconstructing a business on the verge of a receivership. An individual's friends, his relatives, the members of his immediate family, are another valuable asset.

It was the discovery of a resource in relatives that changed entirely the latter course of the lives of two old people. They had reached the years of feebleness and declining strength, and now, alone and apparently friendless, they were living sparingly in two rooms, each with an ever-growing fear of what might happen to the other if he or she were taken first.

The question was not so much one of the physical comforts of life. A home for the aged would have been glad to receive them, or it would have been possible for them to obtain a stipend upon which they could continue to live together, but this would not have solved the problem of their loneliness. They needed to spend their last days among their own kith and kin, and it was relatives that the social case worker, whom they had asked for help, endeavored to find.

The old people had lost all trace of the other members of their family. One clue after another was followed, the search leading first away from the city and then back to it, until at last, within three quarters of an hour's ride on the street car, half a dozen nephews and nieces were found, all living in the same neighborhood.

Years before the old man had violated the ancient family custom by which the great Bible with its history of births, christenings, marriages, and deaths descended to the oldest son. Being the youngest, and coveting the privilege that could not be his by right, he took it by stealth and disappeared. Sometime later he went to live with one of his sisters. Both broke with the rest of the family, and it was not until the social worker was called into consultation that they learned that they were not alone in the world, but that near by there were those to whom they were 'Uncle Sam' and 'Aunt Mary,' and who, the past having been forgiven, would gladly welcome them into their homes.

Resources, then, are the assets a man has outside of himself. They may be economic; they may be spiritual; they may be social. They may be his employer, his lodge, his church, his relatives, his bank account, his university, the municipal employment bureau, the hospital around the corner, his building and loan association. Always they are among the stanchest of the timbers that can be used in helping a person make his adjustments.

Along with the knowledge of them must go the facts which show the influences bearing immediately upon the individual's life. One must appreciate what might be called his setting. Setting may be either a succession of recent events or a present environment which is having a direct effect upon an individual's behavior. His family, his associates at work, the neighborhood in which he lives are all part of his setting. They condition his actions just as what we feel and do in the evening is affected by what has happened and by what we have done during the day.

It was setting which supplied the clue to the unusual behavior of Mrs. Doran. One morning a woman of charming personality called to see her. The two women had had a friendly acquaintance with each other. Nevertheless, no sooner had Mrs. Doran caught sight of her visitor than she picked

up a vase and hurled it at her, and then, pushing
her out of the house, slammed the door upon her.
Considering only the pleasant character of the
visitor and the previous cordial relations which
had existed between her and Mrs. Doran, one
could only conclude that Mrs. Doran was either
vicious or insane. The possession of additional
facts gives the incident its true interpretation.

Mrs. Doran's husband had tuberculosis. He
had been away at a sanatorium, but having become homesick had returned to his family. The
trip and life in the city had been a serious drain
upon his health, and Mrs. Doran saw that he was
steadily losing the strength he had gained in the
mountains. About this time she learned that the
older of her two boys had been infected with his
father's disease and that it would be necessary for
him to take the cure. Application was made for
the admission of Mr. Doran and his son to the
sanatorium, and Mrs. Doran decided that she
would insure their staying away until their disease
was arrested by giving up her home. Her younger
son, Henry, was sent to live with a family in a
neighboring suburb and Mrs. Doran made preparations to store her furniture as soon as the sanatorium could receive the two patients. A month

passed. Twice word was received that there was a place for Samuel, the boy who was sick. Each time on the very day when he was to leave, and after Mrs. Doran had nerved herself to the wrench of separation, notice arrived that his departure would have to be delayed. Meanwhile, Henry seemed to be enjoying his new home so much that his mother began to worry lest in the presence of greater comforts he would forget his parents and his brother.

On the day that Mrs. Doran's visitor called, Samuel's trip to the sanatorium had just been postponed for the third time. Mr. Doran had been venting his own irritation upon his wife and had been abusing her so violently that she had been obliged to take refuge in the cellar where she had spent the night. Morning found her physically and nervously exhausted. Her head ached and she was worried to distraction. She had reached the breaking point.

At this critical time the caller appeared, and with a pleasant smile asked how she was feeling. It was the last straw. To see any other human being cheerful at that moment was more than Mrs. Doran could endure, and she hurled at her visitor the first thing upon which she could lay hands, an understandable action when we know its setting.

Similarly, our attitude toward the man who apparently is listless and uninterested in his work changes when we learn that he is having to stay up most of the night nursing a sick wife. There was a time when truancy was thought to be entirely due to difficulties innate with the schoolboy, difficulties that might be corrected by sending him to a special school, but experience has shown that often the home from which the child comes is chiefly responsible for his trouble. The parents may be discouraging him, they may be ill-treating him, or they may not be taking enough interest in him. In his setting may lie the explanation of his truancy.

Immediate environment and recent events are not always enough to enable one to understand the man in trouble. Sometimes his difficulty lies deeper. Its solution may be determined by his early life and training. Facts of this kind which have to do with the previous, as contrasted with the current history of the individual, social case workers call background.

It was the knowledge of the background of George McKloskey which made possible an understanding of his present difficulties and the helping of him to make a better adjustment.

McKloskey was considered to be a failure by all who were acquainted with him. He had not succeeded in supporting his family. He had never held a job for any length of time. He had made no friends. He seemed, if anything, to avoid his neighbors and his fellow workmen. He complained frequently of feeling tired and worn out. His relatives said that he was lazy, and because he was silent, called him "dummy." Even his wife who loved him dearly began to wonder whether he was not too easily exhausted and whether he ought not to do more for his family. Various attempts were made to solve his problem. None of them was successful. As soon, however, as the background of his life was learned, the way out of trouble became clear.

McKloskey had been born in a small mill town. His mother died when he was still little more than a baby, and his father, a drinking man, married a woman who had seen the bottom of fully as many glasses as he. The child knew little except hard work and abuse. Almost his earliest recollection was that of being kicked into the street by his father with the command that he beg food of the neighbors.

He had not spent a day in school. At nine years he went to the factory that his parents might profit by his wages, and there he worked long hours until he was sixteen. Then he grew weary of the drudgery and hardship of his life and the regularity with which his father appropriated his pay envelope. He ran away from home and came to the city. There he knocked about from one job to another. He had barely passed his twenty-first birthday when he met the girl who a few months later became his wife. Whatever his difficulties in living had been before, they were soon accentuated by the responsibilities of a family, and life became more and more miserable for him and for the household.

Underlying all his experiences were two great emotional facts. He had not gone far past boyhood when he began to suffer from attacks of epilepsy. They were not frequent, but they were always imminent. Sometimes they seized him at work, sometimes on the street. He could never tell where or how they would develop. When he was in the throes of one, his wife seemed better able to take care of him than anybody else, and aside from the fear which he had of them at any time, he dreaded a visitation in her absence. They left him weak and nervously exhausted, so that he had no energy for work.

But he suffered from even a greater handicap. He was illiterate. This was one reason why his jobs were so many and so brief. Sooner or later a situation would develop which would demand an ability to read and he would either be discharged or he would leave through shame. For he was an American of American parentage. If he had been of foreign birth, less would have been expected of him. He would have expected less of himself. Always there was with him this second dread, the dread of the discovery that he could not read. More than the fear of epilepsy it was this which caused him to avoid the company of his fellow workmen. It deprived him of the assurance which every man needs in order to make new acquaintances.

It influenced him in his social life. Several times he had suffered embarrassing disclosures. Once while visiting some friends he was found reading a magazine upside down. On another occasion he had been obliged to confess his inability to tell the time, but the most serious of all the unfortunate incidents that developed from his lack of education happened in Sunday school. Church had been a refuge to him from his troubles. He had found solace and self-expression in religion and he was rarely absent from services.

Then one afternoon in Sunday school the teacher of the Bible class asked him to read a verse of Scripture. McKloskey tried to decline, but the more he demurred the more insistent did the teacher become in encouraging this apparently bashful young man. Finally McKloskey left his seat and walked out of the room, his face ablaze with mortification. That broke his connection with the church.

With each new experience, either of this kind or of an attack of epilepsy, McKloskey's fears grew stronger, until he lost all confidence in himself. He became ashamed of his appearance, although his clothes were no worse than those of many of his neighbors, and in order to avoid being seen he almost never entered his own house by the front door.

Is it surprising that, with such a background of fear and barrenness of opportunity, McKloskey should have been shy, that his jobs were short-lived, and that he made few friends? Yet McKloskey had character; he was not without initiative; he had a substantial asset in the devotion of his wife; both he and she had a sense of humor which enabled them to laugh at the worst of their difficulties; he had a strong and abiding interest in work in the soil — 'the ground is just like a fellow to me,' was how he expressed it. When these and other facts appeared, the way in which McKloskey could find his niche became plain. He needed an environment to which he could feel equal and in which he would have a sense of security and comfort. This sort of environment was found for him in a village of a few hundred people from which he could go to work on a neighboring truck farm, and where there was a simple, friendly atmosphere that after the complicated life in the city made him feel immediately at home.

As in the helping of McKloskey, so with many another person, a knowledge of background may be the determining factor in making possible a readjustment to life. A man is what he has been. He is truly a part of all that he has met and there is no better key to his present than that which he has thought and experienced in the past. If, in addition to knowing a man's background, we know his setting, his resources, and his personal characteristics, we are close to understanding the man himself.

There can, of course, be no final knowledge of human beings and their difficulties, no complete acquaintance with them. Seldom are the depths of personality plumbed, seldom are all experiences disclosed. Personal characteristics, a man's plans for himself, resources, setting, and background, are merely categories under which one can assemble at any given time the facts which he possesses about a man. They make possible a tentative diagnosis, a diagnosis of the situation as it presents itself to-day. To-morrow it may be altered by additional facts; for unlike materials and machines people are forever changing and forever new.

The great essential in arriving at an appreciation of men and women is to remember that all information about human beings is relative and must ever be subject to revision. Then, and then only, are we prepared successfully to apply the four categories that have been described, and thereby to achieve the knowledge and the understanding of other people which are necessary to the helping of them out of trouble.

CHAPTER V

SELF–REVELATION

What is necessary before one can read another's secret? It is not mere curiosity, — we know that shuts up the nature which it tries to read. It is not awkward goodwill; that, too, crushes the flower which it tries to examine.

A man comes with impertinent curiosity and looks into your window, and you shut it in his face indignantly. A friend comes strolling by and gazes in with easy carelessness, not making much of what you may be doing, not thinking it of much importance, and before him you cover up instinctively the work which was serious to you and make believe you were playing games.

When men try to get hold of the secret of your life, no friendship, no kindliness, can make you show it to them unless they evidently really feel as you feel that it is a serious and a sacred thing. There must be something like reverence or awe about the way that they approach you. (*Sermons of Phillips Brooks*.)

THE task even of approximating a knowledge of other people would be impossible were it not for the fundamental need which every human being has for self-revelation. If this is true when the course of life is clear and undisturbed, it is most assuredly true when a man is in difficulty. Then reticence requires an almost conscious effort and confession is often a necessity. There are times when the urge to unburden one's self will not be denied and one is compelled to speak.

The experience that befell a social worker while on a train returning from the seashore is by no means uncommon. A shift in the crowd which filled the aisle of the car — it was the evening of the Fourth of July — placed him opposite a young man who had come on board at the last stop. The man might possibly have been a mechanic. Plainly he was a sturdy, hard-working, self-respecting fellow, not at all the kind of person to air his affairs in public. He asked the social worker when they were due at the terminal and the latter in reply brought forth his time-table. A few minutes later a question about hotels was asked, and answered.

Beyond this there was no conversation. After a quarter of an hour the train approached its destination and the social worker began edging his way toward the platform. The young man followed him, and, as they reached the steps said with a sigh:

"Well, I'm feeling mighty blue to-night."

"That's too bad," the social worker replied. "This isn't a day on which to feel blue."

There was a pause for a moment or two. The train had slowed almost to a stop. Then, the young man continued:

"I've just said good-bye to the best friend I have on earth."

"Oh, I'm sorry," his companion responded. "I'm sorry."

They left the car and started walking down the platform together.

"I'm as much in love with her now as when I married her," the first man remarked; and he began to tell his story. For an hour and a half these two, who until that evening had been strangers to each other, remained in the station while the unhappy husband disclosed the things that were troubling him, many of them of the most intimate character.

He had just left this wife who, he discovered, had been unfaithful to him. The whole tragedy was recent and vivid in his mind and the compulsion to tell was stronger than his natural reticence. The social worker was the first person to whom he happened to speak after leaving home, and to him, therefore, he revealed his distress.

As with this man, so with many people, inhibitions are weakest immediately after an emotional experience. It is then that such persons are most likely to tell what is upon their minds. With others the desire to tell is cumulative in its urgency, until at length they can hold their secrets no longer.

It is indeed, the unusual man who is able to resist the desire to unburden himself, and frequently the price of resistance is a miserable and an embittered personality. People want to tell. When they hesitate, it is only because they wish to be certain that they have found an individual in whom with security they can confide. And by security they mean, not merely safety from a repetition to others of what they have told, or the assurance of action that can be taken to help them, but also the far greater security that comes from the knowledge that they are understood, for people seem almost instinctively to believe, and rightly, that the individual who understands them will guard their secrets and will be able to advise them.

Whatever success a man has in learning to know those whom he is called upon to help rests largely upon whether or not they see in him this capacity to understand. It is the surest introduction to confidences. The person who would possess it must have a fundamental respect for other people. He must feel the unique importance of each individual who approaches him and he must have a faith in human nature that is founded, not upon a sheltered optimism, but upon a knowledge of the facts. "Diogenes," says Chesterton, "looked for his honest man inside every crypt and cavern; but he never thought of looking inside the thief." He who would receive the confession of another man must see honesty in the thief without being blind to his thievery. He must feel neither surprise nor horror at any revelation that may be made to him, no matter how unusual. It is not enough to be silent and to refrain from expressing these emotions. They must not even exist.

He must be impersonal. He must not judge. His attitude toward the person who has revealed himself must not change from what it was before the secret was disclosed. "I told you," explained one woman who had confided to another woman certain things about herself unknown even to her husband, "because I knew that it would not make any difference." It is the capacity to hear the worst or the best in human nature and to accept it neither as worst nor as best, but as life, which is the supreme test of him who would become the confidant of his fellows.

This is by no means an unapproachable ideal. Granted that one has faith in human beings and a liking for them, he can cultivate understanding as he would cultivate any other attitude of mind. It is largely the outgrowth of an enlightened experience in dealing with people in trouble. The man whose first response to abnormalities in the conduct of his neighbor is — "I won't have anything to do with him. His actions are outrageous. He's no good. He doesn't amount to anything" — soon finds his ideas changing when he is faced with the necessity of helping the person of whose behavior he does not approve. Then the conduct which aroused his anger or his disgust becomes a problem to be solved. The more unusual the behavior, the greater he finds the challenge to his ability. He seeks more and more for causes and solutions and, in doing so, obliterates his old prejudices and preconceptions. He begins to appreciate some of the handicaps under which human beings less fortunately placed than himself live; and thus gradually he acquires the attitude and point of view that those in need of help seek in selecting a person to whom to tell their secrets.

Character and personality are not the only introduction to confidences, nor are they alone always enough to encourage self-revelation. Circumstance plays an important part in causing people to tell their secrets, and sometimes seemingly superficial things indicate to people the sort of person who will understand them.

The mere fact that a man is a physician or a social case worker is to many people a guarantee, not simply that they can expect competence and helpfulness, but that they will receive a sympathetic hearing. Certainly no one is entrusted with more secrets than those who follow these two callings. With what difficulty does a physician achieve a vacation. Let it be known that his profession is medicine and the most casual conversation will develop into a revelation of the intimate facts about the life of his vis-à-vis. Similarly the social case worker usually accepts rather than solicits the confidences of those in trouble. The men and the women to whom other men and women may reveal themselves are so few that he whose position or training gives promise of insight and an open mind is singled out for this service.

Of all the circumstances which are taken to indicate the capacity to understand, perhaps the most common is a kinship in experience. One mother will tell another mother what she would be slow to confide to an unmarried person. Members of the same profession, those who have suffered a similar bereavement, men who have faced danger together, have a sense of mutual appreciation that helps them to unburden themselves. How often has one person been heard to say of another, "He's been through it; he knows."

Frequently it is helpful to match what the person in trouble is revealing with a revelation of something in one's own life. It reassures the man in trouble to learn that the handicap or the difficulty which he had thought to be unusual is familiar to others, and that the person who is listening to his story has faced a similar problem. There is a value in the mere sharing of experiences. It gives a person a sense of security to find that his confidant is ready to give of himself as well as to take.

Next, perhaps, to this kinship in experience as a means of helping people to reveal themselves is a kinship in interests.

A social case worker had been called upon for advice about the apparent incompatibility of a husband and wife. Both were Armenians. The woman who had been deserted by the man accused him of neglect, abuse, and non-support. Her relatives endorsed all she said.

It was important that the social worker should learn the man's side of the story. Accordingly she called at the home of a friend of his, also an Armenian.

"I have come to see you," she explained to the woman who answered her ring, "because I am trying to help some friends of yours, Mr. Terian and his wife."

Instantly a mask seemed to fall down over the face of the woman.

"I know nothing," she replied.

It was winter-time and the weather was raw, and so the social worker stepped into the hall saying, "It's a cold day. May I come in for a few minutes?"

Mrs. Demoyan took her visitor into the living-room.

After the two women were seated, the visitor began, "You're an Armenian, aren't you? I have been so interested in Armenia because it has had such a terrible struggle. How long did you live there?"

Simple and obvious though this introduction was, it immediately brought a response. The subject was of the greatest consequence to Mrs. Demoyan, and she began talking about her life in Armenia.

"They have different customs about marriage over there, haven't they?" the visitor suggested after a while.

Mrs. Demoyan replied by saying that she had not known her husband until the day before she was married. She added that Mr. and Mrs. Terian had met each other only five days before their wedding.

A more desirable approach to the purpose of the interview could not have been found. In a very few minutes Mrs. Demoyan had told Mr. Terian's story and had promised to send him to call upon the social worker in order that he might talk with her about his marital difficulties.

Interests are inherently seductive. It is almost impossible to refrain from talking about them once they are suggested, and, as with Mrs. Demoyan, the transition from the impersonal to the more intimate interest takes place almost unconsciously. This is particularly true of the use of reminiscence as a means of learning to know elderly people. The past which they enjoy describing supplies the very background that is essential to him who is trying to understand their problems, and at the same time serves as an introduction to the other facts which it may be necessary to obtain.

There is a value in conversation upon subjects other than the one of immediate importance. It gives the man in need of help an opportunity to become acquainted with the personality of the individual who desires to aid him. While this can be carried to the point at which it becomes a waste of time, there is often no other way of conveying to a person the assurance that here is one with whom he can feel safe. This applies also to doing things together. A lunch, a talk across a restaurant table, an afternoon stroll, may bring forth secrets that no interview in an office could produce. Again and again, the boy or the girl whose reticence has resisted all efforts at conversation has been helped to self-revelation by the influence of an afternoon in a moving-picture show or a ride on a motor-bus.

There is about the doing of things together something which takes from a man the consciousness of being observed. Many people, no matter how much confidence they may place in the person to whom they are talking, prefer not to have him looking into their faces while they speak. To know that he is being noticed reminds a man of himself and makes him self-conscious. If he is seated by the side of his confidant instead of opposite, this sense of being watched does not become so strong. The idea that an individual is more likely to reveal his secrets when he is in the shadow than when he is in the full glare of light is not without its foundation in experience. We want to tell our secrets unobserved even by the person to whom they are being revealed.

Far more important than this in aiding an individual to unburden himself is the demonstration of a friendly interest in him. It was such a demonstration which caused a young unmarried mother to talk to a social case worker about the father of her baby when she had been unable to discuss it with any one else. Instead of seeking an interview upon this subject, the social worker had written a note to the girl asking whether she would not like to enter night school. She knew that the young woman was anxious to learn bookkeeping. When the girl arrived, the conversation was first directed to her new job. She had just obtained a position which gave her an opportunity to work with figures and which greatly pleased and interested her. The question of further training in business was discussed, and plans were made for her admission to an evening high school. Not until then did the social worker venture upon the real subject of the interview.

"Do you feel like talking about Walter, now, Nina?" she asked. Walter was the name of the father of the baby.

The girl began to cry. She had kept her troubles to herself for so long a time, she said, that she had become hopeless. She was relieved to be able to speak about her anxieties. Secure in the friendly interest of the social worker, she told her story.

Sometimes so gradual an approach to the facts is unnecessary and it is possible to go directly to the heart of the trouble.

Two friends who had not seen each other for more than a year chanced to meet on the street.

"How have things been going?" asked the first.

"Fairly well," was the somewhat doubtful reply, and the first speaker, observing a cloudiness about the usually clear and alert glance of his friend, went straight to that which he desired to know.

"Jim," he said, with concern, "are you worried?"

Jim was worried. His friend had opened the door to his story and he laid bare his anxieties.

Even more interesting was the opening question of a physician who was being consulted by an extremely nervous person. She was so excited when she entered his office that she was visibly trembling. The doctor saw his opportunity.

"Are you always as nervous as this?" he asked. Nothing could have been better planned to relieve the patient. By recognizing her difficulty instead of appearing to ignore it, he placed her at once in a free state of mind and soon she was telling him about herself.

The manner in which this first approach is made to the individual in difficulty frequently determines the success of the interview. This is illustrated by the different ways in which two persons set about helping an ex-soldier out of trouble. The soldier had been discharged from a hospital which reported: "There is nothing wrong with the man physically. He seems to be worried about something. Possibly he may be having trouble with his wife."

A young man, a novice in social case work called to see him. Having in mind the statement from the hospital, his greeting to the patient was: "The doctor says you seem to be worried about something. Are you having trouble with your wife?"

The soldier, of course, assured the young man that he had not a worry in all the world and that his wife was a great comfort and help to him. More than this he would not say, and in despair the young man asked a social worker of maturity and experience to see what she could accomplish.

On entering the room, she noticed beside the bed a tray with the breakfast upon it untouched. The soldier lay partly propped by pillows. Tears were rolling down his cheeks.

"Not very hungry this morning," the visitor began, looking at the tray.

The soldier shook his head, but made no reply.

"Well, it's hard to eat when you're not feeling just right," continued the woman. "Were you able to eat any supper last night?"

"Not much," the soldier replied.

"I'm not surprised," said the visitor. "Most men don't like to take their meals in bed. Why don't you ask the landlady to put the tray on the table over there?" — pointing across the room. "Then you could sit up. It would give you more of an appetite."

"I couldn't," replied the man; "I'd be afraid."

"I know," said the social worker understandngly; "you'd feel as if you were going to topple over any minute."

"Yes."

"Especially out on the street, when you're alone. I've had the same feeling myself."

"When you were waiting for the trolley car?" inquired the soldier.

"Yes," answered the social worker, who it happened had had a nervous breakdown. "I used to feel as if I were going to drop. I used to have all sorts of queer feelings."

The soldier showed that he was interested. The tears had stopped.

"What did you do?"

"Just grit my teeth and kept on waiting until the car came."

"What happened?"

"Nothing. After I had stuck it out for a while, the feeling didn't come back." Then, taking a turn at questioning, "Do you find it worse in the morning or at night?"

"Won't you sit down?" the soldier interrupted with a nod toward the chair near the foot of the bed. "It's worse in the afternoon. I always feel weaker then. I guess I get tired by the work at the vocational school. I always feel faint."

"Perhaps you haven't been eating enough for lunch. That's a poor way of economizing — unless one has to," suggested the social worker.

"My Government allowance hasn't been coming regularly," explained the soldier.

Allotments and allowances during and after the war were a subject of interest to every soldier. In answer to a few questions, but largely without suggestion, the young man told when the payments had stopped, how much he had received, how long he had been sick, and when he had been disabled.

"So you see, I haven't always been able to afford lunch," he concluded.

"That's probably a good part of your trouble," the social worker replied. "Three hearty meals a day would make you feel differently. I'll have the landlady send up some hot coffee — I'm afraid this is cold — and some toast. And I'll have her arrange a good lunch and dinner for you. Then you'll feel more like yourself. To-morrow you come and see me and we'll try to do something about your compensation."

The next morning the soldier appeared at her office. The talk had been enough to enable him to master, at least for a time, the neurosis from which he was suffering. Of his own accord, in connection with the plans for obtaining compensation, he remarked that he was sorry not to be able to send money home, and then the fact that he was worried about not being able to support his wife was disclosed, as well as many another fact about himself. Building on this knowledge, the social worker was able to help the soldier to make the adjustments that restored him to health and family.

So it is with most people in difficulty. They want to tell about the things which are worrying them, and if they are only approached in the right way they will disclose their secrets. Trouble seals the lips of few. Usually it compels revelation. Human beings must share their lives with others. Joy is too exquisite, sorrow too bitter, to be endured alone.

"I remember a man," wrote Mrs. Piozzi in her "British Synonymy," "much delighted in by the upper ranks of society in London some twenty years ago, who, upon a trifling embarrassment in his pecuniary affairs, hanged himself behind the stable door, to the astonishment of all who knew him as the liveliest companion and most agreeable converser breathing. 'What upon earth,' said one

at our house, 'could have made —— hang himself?' 'Why, just his having a multitude of acquaintance,' replied Dr. Johnson, 'and ne'er a
friend.'"

Most people want to unburden themselves of
the things that are troubling them. The person
in difficulty may share his secret in part here and
in part there, or he may select some one to whom
he reveals the whole story. In one way or another
he will seek to relieve himself of the load he has
been carrying. All he asks is that his confidant be
a person who will understand him and with whom
he can feel secure.

CHAPTER VI

THE SOURCES OF UNDERSTANDING

Sometimes we speak as if each of us were a single individual, standing solitary, existing alone; but nothing of the sort is true. The smallest conceivable personality is threefold, — father, mother, child. No one of us starts as an individual or can ever after become such, being essentially social, a member merely, a part of a larger whole. (GEORGE HERBERT PALMER in his *Life of Alice Freeman Palmer*.)

No matter how fully and freely an individual may reveal his secrets, he is not likely to be able to present himself as he is. He may describe his thoughts and his feelings, but he can hardly hope accurately to evaluate his capacities and his characteristics, or to appreciate the force of the various influences that are playing upon him. He may consider himself to have certain abilities, while his employer would estimate his talents quite differently. His relations with his church or with his family might show him to be almost another person from the individual he thinks himself to be, while employer, clergyman, and family would differ from one another in the pictures they would draw of him.

To approach an understanding of an individual and his problems one must view him from as many as possible of the major relationships of his life. The chief of these is usually the home. It is here that again and again the answer will be found to many of the difficulties in which a person finds himself. It was in the home that the handicaps which were affecting the adjustment of Martha, the little girl who was silent in school (described in Chapter II), arose, and it was in the home that the solution of the trouble of Mark Sullivan lay.

He had been one of the first men to be discharged when, under the stress of an industrial depression, the F. & M. Company began reducing its force. At one time he had been a capable and an efficient workman, but during more than a year he had been steadily deteriorating. He was sluggish and dull in the performance of his tasks, and he was almost never prompt in arriving at the shop in the morning. It was not surprising that he should have been dismissed.

The social case worker whom Sullivan consulted called at his home. She found it in disarray and confusion. Mrs. Sullivan evidently was a poor housekeeper. It developed that the meals were seldom ready on time and that frequently her husband had been obliged to prepare his breakfast in the morning, pack his lunch, and assume the responsibility for the appearance of dinner on the table at night. No wonder his effectiveness as a workman had been impaired.

One source of difficulty seemed to be Mrs. Sullivan's health. A physician was consulted. His diagnosis pointed to the need of an operation. It was performed, but, although Mrs. Sullivan's general condition showed an improvement, she continued to be as listless and as delicate as before.

Then the social worker became acquainted with Mrs. Sullivan's mother who made her home there. She was an elderly woman, too feeble to be of any assistance in the housekeeping, but not too weak to have a most unfortunate influence upon Mrs. Sullivan. She was one of those people who delight in the discussion of symptoms and who take pleasure in anticipating the worst possible event when any crisis is at hand. It was this characteristic which, with the best of intentions, she had applied to her daughter's state of health. Did Mrs. Sullivan develop the slightest suggestion of a cold, her mother was sure to remark that this was just the most undesirable time of the year to have anything the matter with one; there was so much influenza, or there was so much pneumonia,

or there was so much of some other kind of disease about. A slight loss of color, or quite as read-
ily, a slight heightening of color, would remind
the old lady of the way in which the woman next
door had begun to go down hill the winter she
died of tuberculosis. A stomach ache suggested
cancer. A headache always contained the possibility of mastoiditis. There was scarcely any
change in the bodily condition of Mrs. Sullivan
which did not bring to her mother the message of
serious illness.

In such an environment it would truly have
been a strong will that could have resisted the
temptation to be delicate. It was suggested,
therefore, that a place in a home for the aged be
found for Mrs. Sullivan's mother. This advice
was followed, and Mrs. Sullivan, freed from the
ever-present suggestion of ill-health, began to take
an interest in other things. She regained her
strength. Her housekeeping correspondingly im-
proved, and her husband was able successfully to
meet the requirements of the new job which he
had obtained. Neither Mr. Sullivan nor Mrs.
Sullivan had sensed the cause of their trouble, and
the social worker herself had not discovered it until she had become intimately acquainted with

the life of the family. The key to the problem lay there.

Many similar experiences might be cited as testimony to the importance of the home and the people living in it as a means of developing an understanding of an individual and his adjustments. It is toward the home and the family that the earliest steps — usually the first —- should be taken in seeking an acquaintance with the person in trouble.

Our efforts should not end there. A man's other associates should be consulted. The importance of this is illustrated by the unsuccessful way in which at first the predicament of Esther Hansen was approached and the method by which later an understanding of her difficulty was obtained.

Miss Hansen had asked the father of one of her former schoolmates to lend her three hundred dollars. She was the only support of her parents, both well advanced in years, and of an invalid sister. At a time when houses were difficult to rent, she had been compelled to buy her home or lose it, and now the problem of meeting the interest upon the mortgage had become too great. She had no negotiable assets and no one among her immediate acquaintance to whom she could turn. Very shortly her salary would be increased and the margin which this would yield would enable her to clear her debt in two years.

The presence of the woman, her evident culture, and her anxiety impressed the man. He sent a representative to visit her at her home. Here Miss Hansen made a further explanation of her financial worries. Her parents and her sister and the appearance of the household seemed to substantiate her story, and the loan was made.

After two years Miss Hansen asked the man for a second loan, although she had repaid only a few dollars of the first. A social worker who was consulted decided to talk with those with whom Miss Hansen was associated. The woman was the breadwinner of her family. She had numerous relatives. She was the patient of a physician. She was a governess. She was a subscription agent for a periodical. She had borrowed money from a loan office.

The loan office told a story of money advanced and not repaid. The circulation manager had been greatly annoyed by the complaints he was constantly receiving from persons who had subscribed through her for his magazine and then had received no copies. She had given him neither their money nor their names. The family where Miss Hansen had been employed as a governess reported that she had been away on sick-leave for nearly six months, and even when working she would often appear in the morning and then not return in the afternoon. She was frequently absent without giving any advance notification. The substitute governess said that she had been obliged to go over again with the children whatever ground Miss Hansen was supposed to have covered, for they had learned absolutely nothing. Her physician stated that he had felt justified in defining her trouble as "nervous exhaustion." From the first time he had seen her three years ago, she had been erratic and often irrational. He ascribed her condition to her personal difficulties. She was highly nervous and had a tendency toward hysteria and melancholia.

A visit to Miss Hansen's home had previously disclosed the fact that her mother had died a few months before without having had a physician called. The house had fallen into a state of the wildest disorder and filth. The family possessions were strewn about miscellaneously. Mr. Hansen was a refined but impractical sort of man, well advanced in years, who seemed to be utterly incapable of grappling with the situation. From what he said — and this was later confirmed by the relatives — Miss Hansen's mother had been of unsound mind. The invalid sister had never developed fully either physically or mentally.

The social worker now persuaded Miss Hansen to visit a psychiatrist, who reported that she was suffering from a manic-depressive form of mental disease in which in all likelihood heredity was a factor, and that probably her mental abnormality had been progressing slowly and steadily.

The relatives who were consulted said that they had been puzzled about Miss Hansen and were deeply interested in her. She had never taken them into her confidence, although she had often asked them for money and had always received what she requested. One of the relatives was a lawyer. He immediately offered to take charge of her legal affairs, which were exceedingly involved. He and the other members of the family were eager and willing to help her and her family

Each of the persons who had been associated with Miss Hansen knew only his or her part of the story and was ignorant of the other aspects of her life. Miss Hansen herself had never realized what her financial condition was. She said she had never had the courage to 'face herself.' Nobody, in short, knew the perplexed woman and her difficulties until the social worker, by talking to every one concerned, brought the isolated facts into a connected whole. Had this been done previously, Miss Hansen might have avoided much anxiety and a vast collection of petty debts. The children might have been spared her ineffective teaching, and the relatives might have been rallied immediately to the support and supervision of the household until the time when the two sisters could be admitted to an institution for chronic mental diseases.

The people who were consulted about Miss Hansen occupied a variety of relationships toward her. There were, for example, her physician and the psychiatrist who made possible a better understanding of her mental and nervous condition. Almost everybody has among his associates some one who stands in a professional relationship to him. Most of us if asked about our health could suggest a doctor who would answer this question better than we could. The same thing would be true of our legal affairs, of our relationship to the church, and, with children, of their relationship to school. As with Miss Hansen, so with many other people, it will be found helpful to turn for advice to one or more or all of those who occupy what might be called a professional relationship to the person in trouble.

Closely allied to them are his associates in business. With Miss Hansen this meant the woman who employed her as governess, the loan office, and the circulation manager of the magazine for which she had been selling subscriptions. With another person a different group of people might be consulted, but usually it will be wise to include those who can interpret the vocational and the economic sides of an individual's life.

Even more important are a man's personal relationships, not only his immediate family, but his relatives and his friends. The relatives of Miss Hansen helped both by contributing to the social worker's appreciation of the woman's problem and by assisting in its solution. Sometimes our friends know us more intimately than our kin and are better able to advise us.

There is another source of understanding which in this particular situation it was not necessary to use but which frequently becomes helpful, namely, documents — marriage certificates, burial permits, wills, birth records, deeds of sale. Again and again, when human beings have failed to supply the explanation, the written page has pointed the way to an understanding of an individual. The verification or the non-verification of a marriage may contain the explanation of much that before had not been appreciated, and many a human mystery has been revealed in the ponderous phraseology of a mortgage or the forgotten pages of a will.

It was Miss Hansen herself who told the social worker what persons were touching her life, and she did this in the first interviews that the two women had together. Obviously the earlier one learns about the professional, personal, and business relations of an individual in trouble, the sooner one will be able to help him. Miss Hansen eagerly assented to the suggestion that the social worker make the acquaintance of her associates and see what advice and help they might give. She had confidence in the social worker and understood the point of view from which her difficulty would be considered. Both of these things are important. We must always remember that we are acting for the person in trouble and that the task is far more delicate, far more complicated than a mere gathering of information. One consults other people in order to obtain their advice, in order to learn how they can be of help to the man in difficulty, in order to obtain their position upon the question which is moot, and in order to present the point of view of the individual in trouble. It is out of this manifold service, this entrance into the interplay of relationships that an understanding of the man, of the nature of his adjustment and the circumstances accompanying it is gradually obtained. Let the person in trouble appreciate this attitude in the person who is helping him and he will forward every effort toward communication with those with whom he has been associated.

The friend who seeks to advise a friend has at the outset the advantage of acquaintance and is spared many a step that the stranger must take, but whether friend or stranger, this method of learning to know a man through his family, and through those who stand in a personal, professional, or business relationship to him will be found to be applicable and essential. Sooner or later if one desires to help wisely he will want to consult those whose privilege and right it is to be consulted, and who may both aid in making a

way out of difficulty — and in developing that
understanding of the man in trouble — which,
coupled with his own revelation of himself, is essential to the solution of his problems.

CHAPTER VII

FACING THE FACTS

Thus they went on till they came to about the middle of the Valley, and then Christiana said, "Methinks I see something yonder upon the road before us, a thing of such a shape such as I have not seen." Then said Joseph, "Mother, what is it?" "An ugly thing, child; an ugly thing," said she. "But, mother, what is it like?" said he. "It is like I cannot tell what," said she. And now it was but a little way off; then said she, "It is nigh."

"Well, well," said Mr. Great-heart. "Let them that are most afraid keep close to me." So the fiend came on, and the conductor met it; but when it was just come to him, it vanished to all their sights. (JOHN BUNYAN, *The Pilgrim's Progress*, Second Part.)

THE surest way of overcoming trouble is to face it, squarely and without evasion, is to appreciate what it involves, to recognize it as it is. The worse the predicament, the more perplexing and disturbing, and the more one dreads it, the more important is it that one should reduce it to its elements, that one should analyze and evaluate it. It is the uncertainties, the unknown, the things we do not comprehend, that cause the greatest anxieties. The first step in extricating one's self from difficulty is to determine precisely what the nature of the difficulty is.

Not everybody succeeds always in doing this. As we draw closer to an understanding of the individual in trouble, through the processes described in the preceding chapters, we realize how often there is justification for that homely diagnosis, "he doesn't know what he's up against."

Many people have not enough knowledge of life and of men to grasp the meaning of the events and relationships which are affecting them. They need an interpreter. Indeed, the degree of success or failure with which an individual passes through an experience can almost be determined by the quality and the manner of his preparation for it. This is illustrated by the way in which two girls met a peculiarly difficult situation. Both were fourteen years of age, the daughters of widows. Both widows were about to be confined, and in each instance the baby would be born out of wedlock.

Esther Boardman went to stay with relatives some time before her mother entered the hospital. The words with which the child was welcomed became the text of the conversation during her visit.

"This is terrible. We are all disgraced. Your mother is a bad woman. We're so sorry for you."

Now, whatever distress the relatives may have

felt, their attitude showed a complete failure to deal with actuality. The baby that was about to be born was a fact which no amount of indignation could obviate. No matter what the woman had done, she was still Esther's mother, and the girl would be obliged soon to return to a daily and intimate association with her.

All this the relatives failed to appreciate, and instead of clarifying the situation they only beclouded it with prejudice and rancor, so that when Esther came home she could not tolerate either her mother or the baby. Not for months was she able to reconcile herself to what had happened, and it was only after the death of her little sister a year later that her affection for her mother once more expressed itself.

The second girl, Mary Culvert, happened to spend the period preceding and during her mother's confinement in the home of a woman of rare understanding and discernment. Both in her attitude and in what she said this woman tried to help Mary to face the situation as it was.

"The baby will need you more than most babies would," she explained. "It won't have a father as you had when you were little." She spoke of the difficulties confronting the mother and how she would want the affection of her daughter. There would probably be criticism. It was the more important that Mary should show her mother that no matter what had happened she loved her.

What the woman said helped the girl to appreciate the situation. When she returned home, she exhibited a loyalty to her mother and the baby that was only increased by the unpleasantness of the neighbors, and the difficulty which might have been a means of separating daughter from mother became a bond that drew them closer together.

While in the helping of people out of trouble it can never be said with assurance that any single cause has effected any given result, certainly it was more than a coincidence that in these two histories success should have followed a facing of the facts, and failure a refusal to recognize them.

Various factors entered into the preparation of the second girl for her experience, perhaps the most important of which was that accompanying the explanation of her problem was the description of her mother's need of sympathy and support. There was an appeal to the child's instinct to defend and to protect.

Seldom are the elements in a situation so simple that the bare statement of them is sufficient to enable an individual to face them. Usually much depends upon the manner in which they are revealed. The issue may be determined, as here, by the mood in which the facts are presented or, as with Mrs. Gordon, by the way in which they are ordered and arranged.

Mrs. Gordon had been deserted by her husband. Having followed him to the place where he was now living, she had had several unsatisfactory interviews with him. He had been indifferent and evasive. A social worker sought in vain for a basis upon which the family might be reunited. Mr. Gordon was not to be moved. He regarded his separation from his wife as permanent and his actions more than supported his words.

Inasmuch as the family could not be re-established, it was important that Mrs. Gordon should recognize this and begin making the necessary adjustments. For months she had been living a kind of tentative existence, all her plans being unsettled by the possibility, ever present in her own mind, that her husband might rejoin her. The children had now reached an age at which, for the sake of their education, a degree of permanence in residence was necessary, and they needed interests to take the place of those which under ordinary circumstances their father would have supplied. For their sakes as well as for her own, Mrs. Gordon needed to perceive the situation with which she was confronted.

The social worker set about helping her to do this in an interview which Mrs. Gordon began by saying that she was at a loss to account for her husband's behavior. For two years he had not supported his family. During a large part of this time, to be sure, he had had difficulty in obtaining work, but still he had not even written to her. Her friends felt that there was nothing good in him, but she believed that there must be an explanation. Sometimes it seemed as if the Arthur Gordon she had once known had disappeared.

"Perhaps the best thing to do," the social worker suggested, "would be to start at the beginning and see whether that won't help us to decide what to think."

She already knew much of what Mrs. Gordon would tell her, but she wanted Mrs. Gordon to provide a basis from which her past might be interpreted to her. And so, with the help of a few sympathetic questions, Mrs. Gordon, beginning with her early life, told her story up to the time of her husband's desertion.

She had had a loveless and unhappy childhood. Both her parents had died before she had reached her sixth year and she had been brought up by an aunt who regarded the task as an unwelcome obligation and did not forget to impress this upon her niece. Having lived for a time in the city, the aunt moved to a village where there were no amusements and nothing which interested the girl until Mr. Gordon appeared. He was on a vacation, a good-looking, dashing sort of fellow, apparently ambitious, and with more of an education than Mrs. Gordon had had. He began an ardent courtship. It was the first time since her mother's death that any one had shown her affection. She fell in love with him, and after she had accepted his proposal of marriage he seduced her. She was ignorant of the significance of what she was doing, for she had only the most rudimentary knowledge of the physiology of sex.

A little while later, when the doctor whom she consulted told her that she was pregnant, she believed that she had committed the unpardonable sin. All the background of her religious training seemed to draw in about her and she felt that she was cursed of God.

When Mr. Gordon consented to marry her, she saw him stooping down to lift up a fallen woman and save her from disgrace. Wholly overlooking his greater responsibility, she ever after felt toward him a sense of gratitude which blinded her to his many failings.

After their marriage they went to a city in the Middle West where Mr. Gordon began selling automobiles. Another baby closely followed the first, and, either by reason of her pregnancy or the necessity for taking care of the children, Mrs. Gordon was unable to take part in the social life of her husband, who soon developed a large acquaintance. He told her little about his business, except to say that it frequently necessitated absences from town. Accordingly, she did not worry when he was away from home for a week at a time. At first he had made a point of celebrating the anniversaries of their married life with gifts to her of flowers, or candy, or jewelry. This made an impression upon her that enabled her to overlook many lapses in conduct.

Once a rumor came to her that he was having an affair with one of her friends, but when the

woman assured her that the gossip was without
foundation Mrs. Gordon was glad to be able to
believe her.

Then, Mr. Gordon's sales began to decrease
and the finances of the household went from bad
to worse. Mr. Gordon suggested that he go to a
neighboring city and see whether business would
not be better there. As soon as he had saved
some money, he would send for his wife and children and they would reëstablish their home.
That was two years before. The rest of their experiences the social worker knew.

The story as related here was not the story that
Mrs. Gordon told. Hers was simply a chronolog-
ical recital of events. She did not attempt to
evaluate her history. This the social worker now
undertook to do for her. She began by taking
Mrs. Gordon back over the story which she had
just told.

She explained the connection between Mrs.
Gordon's loveless childhood, her ignorance about
sex, and her seduction by Mr. Gordon. She
showed her the part her aunt's insistence had
played in Mr. Gordon's willingness to marry her,
the insincerity of her husband's absences from
home while he was still nominally living with his

ıamily, and how the woman who had denied any entanglement with him had deceived her. Then she helped Mrs. Gordon to see the significance of her husband's silence during the two years of his desertion.

The social worker was simply interpreting to Mrs. Gordon out of her own words the experiences through which she had gone. It was Mrs. Gordon who made the diagnosis. There seemed to be no other explanation, she said, except the one that her husband no longer cared for her. The social worker pointed out that perhaps he did not have the capacity for real affection. This might be either a temporary condition or a permanent handicap. It was also possible that there might be some one else whom he loved.

The ultimate fact, that Mrs. Gordon could not hope to be reunited with her husband and that upon her would fall the responsibility of making decisions for her children, was not mentioned, although, of course, it was present by implication. It would be enough for her to start by considering whether or not her husband loved her.

Mrs. Gordon then had an interview with Mr. Gordon which showed how much she had profited by the discussion of her problem. She said that she had never realized that she could talk so frankly with him. They had gone over things together from the beginning, just as she and the social worker had done.

Mr. Gordon told his wife that he would lie to her no longer. He admitted that his love had never been anything but physical. He said that she "would have to go on without him except for financial support" which he realized he must supply. Thus, he himself confronted his wife with the adjustment which she must eventually make.

Neither this interview nor the one with the social worker was alone enough to cause Mrs. Gordon to accept the possibility of a permanent separation from her husband. The great revolutions in life are not so easily gone through with as this. These two interviews were just the beginning of her recognition that her home would have to be built upon a different basis. It required many weeks and the continued indifference of her husband to establish the inevitable finally in her mind and in her plans; but it was the revealing interview with the social worker that supplied the foundation for an understanding of what her life had been and the nature of the adjustment she must make.

The procedure followed in this interview is frequently used in helping people out of trouble, and particularly, in helping them to understand and to face their problems. The process by which an individual tells the story of his experiences and then has that story retold to him as it appears to the person whom he has consulted is a fundamental method of interpretation. The application of it will vary with circumstances but the same underlying principle is always involved.

The initial telling serves two purposes — it usually relieves the feelings of the person in trouble, preparing him emotionally for the reception of the truth and it makes his history vivid. He sees his life as a whole and is thus the better able to appreciate the significance of its events and relationships as they are revealed to him. Sometimes the mere act of reciting the facts clarifies his mind so that by the time he has completed his story he is well on the way to an understanding of it. Sometimes, also, the process of telling and of receiving a sympathetic hearing strengthens his confidence in the person who is listening to him and by that much facilitates the task of interpretation.

The retelling of the story is not necessarily a

literal rehearsing of the entire narrative. While occasionally it is precisely this, more often it becomes rather a series of questions, suggestions, and comments which clear away the clouds of difficulty and discover the problem in its essentials.

Presumably the person who is able to help brings to the work of interpretation the background of a wider experience in the adjustment at hand than that possessed by the individual in trouble. This is an important consideration. It is what influences us in consulting a physician when we are ill. We seek an explanation of certain pains and disabilities through the medium of his greater knowledge of disease. It may be the first time that we have encountered this particular pain. To us it is unique. To him it is familiar, a symptom which he has observed in many different people. So, too, the trouble which puzzles a man can often be clarified by the experience of one who has seen other persons pass through the same difficulty.

When William Flack lost his job, although through no fault of his, he felt a sense of failure and defeat. He began to have doubts about himself. He was ashamed. He dreaded the inevitable question about what he was now doing. He wanted to avoid meeting his friends. He was loath to mention his predicament. Finally, he sought the advice of a person who had helped many men through the difficulties of unemployment. This man told him that he was simply showing what were characteristic symptoms of his adjustment. They were almost inevitable accompaniments of his problem and nearly everybody in a like situation was obliged to cope with them. The cure lay in admitting his predicament and in recognizing that only as he informed people that he was in the market for a job would he be likely to secure employment. The relief that William Flack felt in learning that his reactions to his problem were not unique is the relief which one can bring to many an individual who is in difficulty by giving him the perspective that comes from knowing what other people have felt and done under the same circumstances.

The interpretation of this man's problem was accomplished through a marshaling of testimony about what had occurred in many similar problems. For Mrs. Gordon it involved reviewing her own intimate experiences with a person who not being involved in them was able to point out their significance to her. With the daughter of the widow who was about to become a mother it required a statement of the facts accompanied by an appeal to the child's sympathies and to her instinct to protect.

With each individual there was a difference in procedure, but it all led to the same conclusion — the facing of the facts. This is not an easy thing for anybody to do. It takes courage. Often one is tempted to follow the example of the boy who plays hookey to avoid taking an examination, even though the postponement only prepares a more unpleasant crisis. Often, too, like Christiana in the Valley of the Shadow of Death, we are glad to have some one stand with us as we confront the experience. Yet not infrequently to face the adjustment strips it of much of its terror. To see what one is about to meet or what one is already grappling with is to be strengthened for overcoming it. Let a man face the facts of his life and he has gone more than halfway toward a solution of his problems. The surest way out of trouble will be found in a seeking of the truth.

CHAPTER VIII

INTERPRETATION

Who hath sailed about the world of his own heart, sounded each creek, surveyed each corner, but that there still remains therein much terra incognita to himself? (THOMAS FULLER, *The Holy and the Profane State.*)

Lord, and how some of us do imagine ourselves misunderstood, when the trouble is that we are understood by others, but not by ourselves. (F. P. A., "The Diary of Our Own Samuel Pepys," *New York World*, October 30, 1922.)

WERE our difficulties as wholly apart from ourselves as a problem in arithmetic the facing of them would be a simple matter. But they are not. Often the most critical fact in a man's life is himself and frequently the diagnosis, "He doesn't know what he's up against," must be accompanied by the equally familiar one, "He's his own worst enemy."

He may be unskillful in handling himself. He may have unfortunate mannerisms. He may say the wrong thing in spite of his desire to say the right. He may have habits that are as hobbles to his efforts toward success. He may not appreciate his own worth. He may lack confidence in his ability. He may be making mistakes in behavior.

He may not realize that in order to adjust himself to life he must change himself.

It is rarely that in greater or less degree a man's personality is not involved when he comes to face the predicament that is troubling him. To tell the unemployed man (see Chapter VII) that his sense of failure and of shame was a symptom of his unemployment was in a measure interpreting him to himself. After all, the real cause of his worry was lest there be something wrong with him. To learn that his difficulty was typical of what many other persons had suffered was to be assured that he was not peculiar in this respect and that, therefore, he was as good a man as he had ever been. His concern was himself, but to talk to him in terms of his adjustment was to make his problem objective rather than personal and thus to render it easier for him to grasp.

For, although since our earliest school days we have been reared to believe the maxim, 'Know Thyself,' we find the acquiring of this knowledge through the vehicle of other people the most painful of all ordeals. Few of us can receive the slightest compliment without blushing or undergoing a change in facial expression, and when the truth carries an adverse criticism our suffering is so great that we cannot recall what was said without feeling a repetition of the anguish we endured at the time.

The pain of such experiences causes us to try in every way possible to protect ourselves from a recurrence of them. We will shy with all the timid alertness of a frightened animal from anything which appears to be leading us into this kind of a discussion. Once we are unavoidably in the midst of it we take various means of saving ourselves from hurt. Some people do this by pleasantly admitting everything that they are told, thus shortening and lightening the ordeal and escaping the unpleasantness of any extended thought upon the subject. Others surround themselves with an armour of temper, and through a quick anger prevent themselves from perceiving the truth that may disturb them. Others again guard themselves by unconsciously cultivating such an attitude of certainty about their qualities and characteristics that it is practically impossible for them to apprehend or to believe anything which contradicts their own opinion of themselves. Sometimes people reduce the discomfort of the experience by discounting the capacity of the individual who is presenting the truth to them. What, after all, does he know about it, and what right has he to speak as he does. He has failings of his own — and thus thinking, they avoid or relieve any injury to their feelings.

Some people develop a too great willingness to engage in discussions about themselves and their problems. Just as not infrequently a sick person who has dreaded the thought of an operation comes to like the life of the hospital so much that he acquires what the doctors and nurses speak of as hospitalitis, and will even, for the sake of returning to the institution, complain of symptoms which require a surgeon, so, too, some individuals having had the experience of an exposition of themselves will seek a repetition of that experience at every opportunity. Nothing delights such an individual more than a description of himself as this or that sort of man, even though the criticism be of a derogatory nature. He likes to think of himself as a case to be studied, but in spite of the advice he receives he makes no effort to change. Once the initial sensitiveness to criticism has been dulled, this is a state of mind into which almost anybody can fall. The individual who is thus afflicted becomes so much interested in thinking about himself that he loses the habit of

action and becomes an ineffective human being,
useless both to himself and to others.

The interpretation of a man should not, therefore, be undertaken without some assurance that
he will be able to profit by it. Usually one will do
best to wait until the person in trouble asks for
this service. His request may be direct or implied.
That it is spoken may not, however, necessarily
mean that it is intended. A man may ask for advice about himself when he is too overwrought to
apprehend what may be said to him. He may
urge that he be told the truth when it is not the
truth that he wishes to hear. What he desires to
be told is that in his attitude and behavior he is
being the only sort of person he could be under
the circumstances. On the other hand, often
those to whom we long to tell the truth know it
before we speak, and when we tell them that which
we think is new to them we are only confirming
what they have long suspected. On every count
the burden of proof rests upon the person who
feels that he must offer to help a man to face the
facts about himself.

What this process of interpretation involves
when once it is called for may be seen in part in
the story of Salvatore Donato.

Donato was a violinist of fair ability, but a fondness for liquor, unwisely indulgent parents, and a wife whose standards of home-making were below his own, had contributed to his deterioration. For fifteen years he had slipped from one failure to another until at last he was going about the streets seeking alms in return for his music. Even in this he was unsuccessful, and at length his wife and his five children and he were reduced to living in three miserable rooms. They faced a winter without money for fuel and with no apparent means of paying the rent now overdue or of providing the next day's food. Donato's parents had come to the rescue on so many similar occasions that they were unwilling to help, and Mrs. Donato appealed to a social agency.

A social case worker called upon the family in the late afternoon and found Mr. and Mrs. Donato and their children sitting in semi-darkness. There had been no money with which to buy oil. Before entering the house the social worker had obtained from Mr. Donato's father, and from several other persons a general knowledge of the situation and of Mr. Donato's difficulties.

"If I am to be of any help to you," she began, "I shall need certain information." She drew a chair close to one of the windows, and, departing from her usual practice, put her inquiries to Mr. Donato in almost questionnaire form, entering the answers upon a pad. She was as impersonal in her manner as a physician would have been in inquiring about symptoms. She asked the name of his present employer — he had none; his last job — he had had none for years; his vocation; his means of livelihood; his early successes; his membership in an orchestra; and so on through his life. In this the social worker was making a different application of the same method as that illustrated in the interview with Mrs. Gordon (see Chapter VII). Through her questions she was taking Donato back from the present to the past and helping him to tell himself what he had been. She made no attempt to evaluate the facts which were being set forth. She accepted them without comment. Everybody else who had dealt with Donato had berated him, had told him that they were disgusted with him, and in similar ways had expressed their scorn, arousing within him protective emotions which prevented him from appreciating the truth of what they said.

Having led him to recapitulate his life she looked up from her notes: "Now, tell me, Mr. Donato," she asked, "what is the trouble?" Her manner of speaking was one of consideration and respect. The interview thus far had enabled her to recognize in him that which his parents and even his wife had forgotten. Along with the signs of weakness she saw a certain sensitiveness and something akin to fineness. Not for years had any one addressed this side of his nature.

"It is as you see," he replied sadly. "We are at the end." He was seated opposite to her.

She leaned toward him. "It is terrible for you to be living like this," she said in a tone low enough to reach his ears alone. Other people had told him what they thought about him in voices loud enough to inform the whole neighborhood. "You played in an orchestra, and now" — she hesitated — "you beg."

That sentence brought the whole picture into focus.

"The more I thought about it, the more ashamed I felt," Donato told a friend to whom some months afterward he described the interview. The social worker had succeeded in enabling him to see himself. The remainder of the interview was only a confirmation of her accomplishment.

"But what can I do?" Donato was apologetic. "I have no money. I have pawned my violin."

"You can work."

"My leg," he replied; "I am lame. No one would take me."

"You can get a job here," the social worker told him, scribbling the address of an employment bureau upon her card. "I'll see that you have a better pair of shoes," she added, noticing the condition of those he was wearing.

The effect of the interview was more instant than she had realized. Although she called early the next morning with the shoes, Donato had gone to the employment bureau in a pair of leather slippers — it was crisp winter weather — and had secured a job as a laborer, a place that he held for six months until it was possible for him to return to music as a vocation instead of as an introduction to alms.

There were several reasons for the social worker's success. In the first place, she acted from a well-founded knowledge of the man, obtained from his parents, his physician, and others who had tried to help him. It was this knowledge which made it possible for her to point the interview as she did. There is a vast amount of harm done by well-intentioned people who in a first interview with a stranger give him advice which rests upon nothing but the impression they have gotten of him in the course of this initial conversation.

The atmosphere of impersonality which the social worker cast about the interview was another factor in her success. By approaching Donato objectively, by not evaluating what he told her or commenting upon it until she spoke the critical sentence in which she compared his present beggary with his happier past, she prevented the rising of beclouding emotions. The impartial and unbiased way in which she addressed him took him in a sense outside of himself and enabled him to see Donato as he was.

This attitude of impersonality is exceedingly important. Usually, as with Donato, the person in trouble has passed through that trying stage when relatives and neighbors take sides for and against him, blaming or condoning, chiding or sympathizing, until his feelings have become oversensitized to any discussion of himself. The objectivity of a stranger is like the application of the antiseptic solution that cleans the infected wound.

The very intimacy of our relations with the members of our families and with other friends makes it difficult for them to help us to face the facts about ourselves. We are too cognizant of their limitations and their weaknesses to give weight to what they say. It not infrequently happens that the more dearly we love them the more animus we seem to find in what, with every good intention, they tell us about ourselves. This is not to say that often the best person to reveal the truth to a man is an intimate friend, but it does mean that the chances for success rest with the individual whose relationship with him is distinctly an impersonal one.

In such a relationship stand the psychiatrist, the teacher, the physician, the social worker, the lawyer, the clergyman, the employer. In varying degree and under different circumstances these occupy a position of authority. Their place, their experience, and their special knowledge give us confidence in them. Their opinions have credit with us. With them we can develop a kind of oblique objectivity. We can receive the truth from them with less hurt because we feel that it is not our whole selves that we are presenting for review but only that part of us which is student, employee, parishioner, patient, or client.

There is also that in our relationship with them which in our minds seems to vest them with the right and the duty under suitable circumstances to tell us that which we need to know about ourselves. Donato did not specifically ask the social worker to show him the facts about himself, but he instinctively recognized the appropriateness of her doing this. In seeking medical advice the patient realizes that the state of his health may make it necessary for his physician to discuss with him his most intimate habits. It is taken for granted that a teacher may discover in the quality of a student's work a need for helping him to perceive mistakes in behavior, and it is generally understood that at the time of employment, of promotion, of discharge, and in many other situations an employer may find it important to give an employee an estimate of his personality and work.

It is a question whether often under such circumstances the employer does not owe his employee this service, provided, of course, he recognizes in him an attitude of mind which will enable him to accept what he is told. For to be able to receive the truth requires the capacity for impersonality in the person who is being helped as well as in him who is helping. There are few tributes to character that are higher than that which is paid a man when an employer takes his open-mindedness for granted by telling him why he is not offering him the position for which he has applied or why he is not promoting him. Some executives go farther than this, and as a matter of routine give each member of the staff an opportunity once or twice a year to learn how he and his work are regarded. This practice, applying as it does to everybody, throws an atmosphere of impersonality about the whole process and smooths the way to a reception of the truth.

The truth is as important as the impersonality. This is frequently forgotten. Too often we are inclined to speak in the spirit of Mrs. King, of "Old Chester Tales," who told people things flatly and frankly for their own good out of a sense of duty. To interpret a man to himself is to set forth not merely that which is unfavorable. This sort of half-truth only hurts and blocks him. It is the balanced presentation that wins a hearing.

The social worker told Donato the whole truth. She referred to the unfortunate elements in his character but she also recognized his strengths. That she herself was a musician helped her perhaps the more quickly to sense his possibilities, but to use one's every resource is part of the art of helping people and does not vitiate the principle that in explaining a man to himself it is important to set forth his assets as well as his liabilities. Emphasis at the start upon his positive qualities strengthens him for learning about his weaknesses. The consciousness that he is appreciated for his successes enables him to consider his failures in a hopeful and constructive spirit.

This method of interpretation prepares the way for the next process which is exemplified in the interview with Donato. Having, through the recognition of his ability, aroused within him the desire to change, the social worker offered him an opportunity to act. She made the concrete and practical suggestion that he take a job. Without something definite to do, something to work toward, any discussion of a man with himself is likely to encourage a morbid introspectiveness that defeats the very end we would accomplish. The way men change is by following thought with action, and in offering opportunity for the one it is important to offer opportunity for the other.

Action, a balanced presentation, impersonality,

these three things underlie the process of explaining a man to himself. They apply also to the interpretating of his adjustments to him and to many other phases of the art of helping people out of trouble.

In one respect the story of Donato is not typical. His change was far more immediate than usually happens. Most people arrive at an understanding of themselves only gradually. It is a slow dawning rather than a sudden flash.

Self-knowledge is a triumph of intelligence over emotion, but such victories do not come quickly. Human beings surround themselves with such a network of sensitiveness that any close approach to their personalities is often impossible. Frequently one must try to accomplish by indirection what one would prefer to bring about through more direct methods. One must explain adjustment after adjustment, in the hope that at last by implication the individual may come to realize that the fundamental difficulty lies in himself. Sometimes he can be helped to self-understanding through an interpretation to him of those who are involved in his adjustment. Sometimes one must give up hope of interpretation by any means and must rely instead upon quickening his desires and extending his interests and upon other phases of the art of helpfulness. It must be remembered that the facing of a man with the facts about himself is a method, not an end, a method fraught with difficulty and to be adopted only when there is good assurance of success. The surest way out of trouble is the recognition of the truth, but those that achieve this are exceedingly few.

CHAPTER IX

MEDIATION

What, then, is our neighbor? Thou hast regarded his thought, his feeling, as somehow different from thine. Thou hast said, 'A pain in him is not like a pain in me, but something far easier to bear.' He seems to thee a little less living than thou; his life is dim, it is cold, it is a pale fire beside thy own burning desires. . . . So, dimly and by instinct hast thou lived with thy neighbor, and hast known him not, being blind. Thou hast made [of him] a thing, no Self at all. (JOSIAH ROYCE, *The Religious Aspect of Philosophy*.)

INASMUCH as few people are solitary, most persons being framed in a vast variety of relationships, having families, homes, neighbors, and many other affiliations, there is nothing more important to success in living than an appreciation of our fellows or more fraught with trouble than a failure to understand them. Blindness to the thoughts and desires and feelings of others seems, nevertheless, to be a common human trait. It is at the bottom of many a maladjustment. It appears again and again as a disturbing factor in marriage, in widowhood, in adolescence, in work, in single life. Nearly everybody has at some time been called upon to repair the damage which it has caused.

The remedy lies, obviously, in clearing away

whatever misunderstandings exist. It is a work of interpretation, of mediation, and often of arbitration, the underlying principle always being the explanation of one person to another, as, for example, Mrs. Reynolds was explained to her husband.

He was out of patience with her. There had been trouble between them for many months. She was insanely jealous of him and without cause accused him of being unfaithful to her, even going to the hospital to see whether a woman, who was ill there, a fellow employee of his had not supplanted her in his affections. She mistrusted that he was withholding part of his wages from her, as indeed he was, and the disturbance which she made at his place of employment was undoubtedly a factor in bringing about his discharge. When he learned that he had lost his job, he took some money which had come to him as part of a legacy and gave himself up to alcohol. He had not been home for several days when the following interview took place.

"I suppose I am to blame for it all," he began sullenly. "I have done all sorts of things, I suppose, with no cause at all."

"I am neither blaming nor praising you," the

social case worker replied. "If I did I wouldn't have asked you to come to my office and tell your story."

"Oh, what's the use of my talking," Reynolds retorted unconvinced. "My wife's been black-guarding me to you."

"Now, Mr. Reynolds, you know that I know too much about your situation to be influenced by anything that anybody might say to me, but I can only help you if you will lay your cards down on the table and be fair with me."

"Oh," he exclaimed. "I admit that I've been drinking. Any man would have if he'd been through what I've been through. You take a horse out and beat it and he will act ugly toward you. It's the same way with a human being. If she would only have a little faith in me and speak a kind word to me once in a while, I could go ahead and keep things decent."

"I know it's been hard for you," he was assured, "but your wife has a pretty hard time of it too. She's at home all day working. She scarcely sees anybody except the children and they're a good deal of a trial. Anybody would be nervous with five of them running in and out all day long."

"Yes, but she needn't criticize me to them.

Why, she even sent Sarah to Fifteenth Street to watch where I went from the factory. The way she talks to me, the children don't respect me any more."

"If you heard how nicely Harry talks about you, you wouldn't think so," the social worker replied. "And, after all, you did tell your wife that your wages were less than they were. That's why she sent Sarah."

"And last pay-day she came herself," Reynolds interrupted, "and made such a fuss that I lost my job."

"She told me all about it," explained the social worker. "She knows that she was responsible for your discharge. She is very sorry. She said so to me several times."

Reynolds was mollified by this. He seemed pleased that his wife had admitted her mistake. "Only I wish she had told it to me," he remarked, and added that it was the loss of his job and Mrs. Reynolds's belief that he had been unfaithful to her which had driven him to drink.

"If it hadn't been for her going to the hospital to see Miss Arsen, I wouldn't have gone on a spree. Miss Arsen is fifty, if she's a day. The only time I ever saw her was at the factory, except when she first got sick. Then I took her pay to her house. But I had nothing else to do with her, and when my wife went out to the hospital to see her and asked for the maternity ward, that was the last straw."

"Your wife told me about that too." Reynolds stared at the social worker in surprise. "And I think she really feels badly about it and is ashamed."

The man was amazed and appeased by this, too much so to reply, and the social worker continued:

"A good deal of your wife's trouble is caused by her nervousness. People are just like the machines you run at the steel works. Some of them are more complicated and harder to understand than others. If you don't handle them properly, they break and do a lot of damage. When you have a machine you don't understand, don't you try one way and then another until you find the one that works? Think how much time and patience you take over a machine of steel. And how much more complicated human beings are!"

"That's true," the man admitted. "That's true. She is nervous and I guess she does have a hard time. Well, she seems to know what's what now and I'll do the best I can if she will do her part." Then, as he rose to go, he added:

"It's easy for me to keep from drinking. You won't catch me going on another spree now."

He kept his word. Moreover, he made an earnest effort to understand and to conciliate his wife, and it was only her mental condition which ultimately caused them to decide upon a separation as the one possible solution.

In this interview the social worker did three things. She told Mr. Reynolds that his wife recognized her mistakes and was sorry for them. At the same time she did not let him forget that he had not been truthful about his wages. When errors have been made, it is usually wise to dispose of them by admitting them. This clears the way for a new understanding. It would have been better if Mrs. Reynolds could have done this for herself, but, since she could not, there was an advantage in having the social worker act for her, inasmuch as she could point out to Mr. Reynolds wherein he too had been wrong, a task which his wife could scarcely have undertaken without jeopardizing the chances of a better relationship.

The next step consisted in showing Mr. Rey-

nolds some of the difficulties which were handicapping his wife. There is no more certain way of
bringing about an understanding of an individual
than to describe the obstacles with which he or
she must contend. It awakens sympathy and also
explains the reasons for actions of which otherwise there would be adverse criticism.

Lastly, the interview was clinched by the
analogy of the machine and the human being.
This was an attempt to interpret Mrs. Reynolds
in terms of Mr. Reynolds's own experience. It
was an application of that fundamental principle
in education which advises one to proceed through
the known to the unknown.

Throughout the interview, of which what has
been quoted was only a part, the social worker did
not fail to give a sympathetic hearing to all that
Mr. Reynolds said, even when she was obliged to
tell him that she could not agree with him. By
the time he left her office he had relieved himself
of the emotions which had prevented him from
thinking clearly about his predicament. To allow
an angry man "to have his say" is the surest
method of bringing him to reason. Feelings dis-
sipate themselves in their own explosion, but ac-
cumulate in violence as they are forced back by

antagonism, a law of human nature which every one recognizes in the abstract, but which few observe when the emotional outburst is directed against them or when it is their part to listen to it.

Another important phase of interpretation consists in showing what might be called the average expectation of human beings. This was what Mrs. Cavallo needed to know in order to understand her son, Tony, who ran away from home one day taking with him twenty dollars which she had set aside for the payment of the rent.

"Tony no good — too bad," Mrs. Cavallo complained. "I treat him right. I give him clothes. I give him money for lunches. I give him car-fare."

"That's just the trouble," explained the social worker. "You give him only the money he has to have. You must remember Tony is growing up. He wants a good time, wants to do as other boys of his age do. He sees other boys going to the movies and he wants to go too."

Mrs. Cavallo raised another objection.

"I sit here. I sew all day, all night. He stay out nights, no come in."

"How late?" asked the social worker.

"Sometimes half-past nine, sometimes ten o'clock."

"That's not so bad," Mrs. Cavallo's visitor assured her. "If a boy of sixteen is in by ten o'clock, that's early enough."

"Tony no good, though," returned the mother, shaking her head. "He steal twenty dollars that I save for house [meaning rent] and coal."

"How did you get the twenty dollars?" her visitor inquired.

"Tony give me his pay every week. I save twenty dollars."

"Well, then," the social worker explained, "Tony probably didn't think that he was stealing the money. He thought it belonged to him. He had earned it. You mustn't expect a boy of his age to feel the same responsibility toward the family that you do."

But Mrs. Cavallo found still another objection.

"Tony just like his father. He no good."

"If Tony has had as bad a father as you say, how do you expect him to support you like a good husband?" was the response. "He hasn't had any example to live up to."

"He talk like his father," continued Mrs. Cavallo, still apparently unconvinced. "He talk bad to me. When I tell him to do something, he talk bad. He say — 'I do as I darn please.'"

"He's always heard his father talk that way," the social worker reminded the mother. "Besides, he thinks he has the right to do as he pleases because he earns his own money."

Thus far Mrs. Cavallo had shown no indication of any appreciation of Tony's side of the argument, except to change the subject after each of the social worker's comments. Now, however, she said:

"A friend tell me my husband say Tony come over there to see him. You, please, go over and see my husband and Tony."

"Will you take Tony back?" the social worker asked.

"Yes," answered Mrs. Cavallo, evidently from a variety of motives. "No good for Tony to be over there. We need Tony."

"Will you give him money from his pay and let him have a good time two or three nights a week?"

"Yes, I do that."

The social worker, having progressed thus far in helping the mother to a more reasonable attitude toward her son, now went to see the father, who was separated from his wife and was living in a neighboring city. Mr. Cavallo promised to tell

Tony to call to see the social worker, but Tony did not do so. She, therefore, went once more to see Mr. Cavallo, this time in the company of Mrs. Cavallo, who had several matters of business to transact with him. They found father and son together.

The interview that ensued was decidedly to the advantage of the mother. The man was considerably older than the woman, as lifeless and careless as she was energetic and neat. He was not well, and doubtless his irritability was partly due to this cause, but he stormed about needlessly while his wife was quiet and dignified. All the differences that had existed between the two appeared in the discussion and the substantial qualities of Mrs. Cavallo became more and more evident.

The social worker had not planned the interview as a demonstration for Tony, but since it was developing in this way she allowed the boy to watch his parents for a few minutes. Then she took him aside.

"Well, Tony," she said, "I have heard something about this trouble that you and your mother have had, and I'd like to hear your side."

Tony was moody and sullen, but also a bit ashamed.

"I got tired of giving all my wages to her and hearing her talk," he grumbled.

"Why did she scold you?" the social worker asked.

"She didn't think I ought to go out with the fellows. She didn't want me to go to the movies."

"It was only her desire to do the best for you," the social worker explained. "She meant well. You know that boys sometimes get into trouble by hanging around the streets at night."

"She wouldn't give me my money," Tony objected.

"That was because your mother thought the money could be better spent at home. She has to think of the whole family. You want your sisters to be well dressed, don't you? You ought to be proud because she wants to have nice things and because she keeps the house so clean and neat." The social worker now made a direct plea to the boy. "She's lonely without you. She needs some one at home to protect her. If you will come back, she has promised to give you spending money and to let you go out at night."

Tony was plainly appeased by what the social worker told him, but he was too stubborn to yield at once.

"Well, I'll think it over," was all he would say. But a few days later he visited his mother and within two weeks he was at home.

In addition to explaining the son to the mother in terms of what boys ordinarily want and do, and the mother to the son in the light of her responsibility as a parent, the social worker in bringing about a better understanding also acted as a negotiator and mediator. She proposed a new working agreement to Mrs. Cavallo and submitted it to Tony. It was a situation in which concessions must needs be made by both. It was a mutual adjustment.

Peter and Annie Ainsley, on the other hand, represent the type of problem in which the adjustment of a family depends chiefly and almost exclusively upon the actions of others. Their relatives had consulted a social worker in order to discover why Peter could not secure a better job and why Annie did not take better care of her home. They could not understand why she did not serve meals at regular hours; why her husband's clothes were never mended; why her little daughter was not started for school early enough to enable the child to arrive there on time, and why, when the family moved into a new home, the furniture remained for days exactly where the moving men had left it.

The social worker, having taken the man and the woman to a mental clinic, suggested that the relatives meet for a conference with her. There were ten adults in the group that gathered one evening at the home of Mr. and Mrs. Gardner, the parents of Mrs. Ainsley. All the brothers and sisters of the man and the woman were present. They had brought their children with them and every now and then the discussion was interrupted by the entrance of one or another of the youngsters.

"I am not going to try to repeat the doctor's exact words," the social worker began, for she knew her audience was composed chiefly of persons of no great education. "But it amounts to this: Peter and Annie have never grown up mentally. Their bodies are fully developed and they have the feelings of a man and a woman. They have fallen in love with each other and have married like the rest of you, but their brains are still those of a boy and a girl. Their minds haven't changed since they were seven or eight years old."

Just then one of the children looked in through the door for a moment and then ran away.

"Suppose Esther were suddenly to be given a great big grown-up person's body to manage," the social worker suggested after the little girl had left, "and suppose she were to have all the grown-up person's responsibilities; the marketing, taking care of the children, finding a new house, planning the meals, and all the other things, wouldn't she make many of the same mistakes that Annie makes? As Esther's body gets older, her mind will grow older too. She will be able to think what to do. She will learn by experience. But Annie so far as her mind is concerned is just where Esther is to-day. She always will be. The same is true of Peter. He and Annie aren't able to decide things for themselves."

"Why, that isn't the way Annie is at all," interrupted one of the sisters. "She knows perfectly well what she wants and she knows how to holler for it too. She certainly can make an uproar if she has a mind to."

"Doesn't that almost prove what I said?" the social worker replied. "Isn't that just the way children act? Surely hollering or making an uproar would not be your or my way of obtaining our wishes."

The company smiled, and the speaker continued:

"Children know what they want, but they don't always want the right things. We expect adults to decide rightly most of the time at least."

The family was plainly convinced of this point and she turned to another phase of the same question.

"When Annie still lived at home, was she interested in a lot of different things or did she seem to be 'hipped' on only one thing?"

"Oh, my," exclaimed the sister who had spoken before, "I guess she was 'hipped' all right. She used to be crazy about cleaning and wouldn't even let father sit on any of the chairs after she had dusted. If he did, she'd almost throw a fit. Really, I don't know what's come over her lately, but since the baby came she hasn't cared a bit about anything else."

"Nothing has come over her," the social worker explained. "She simply hasn't the ability to be interested in the many things you can be interested in. She has room for only one interest. Before she was married, she cleaned. After her marriage she wanted furniture and spent all her money for it. When the baby came she did nothing but take care of him and everything else had to go — cleaning, furniture, Peter, marketing, everything."

Old Mr. Gardner shook his head.

"Yes," he said, "I knowed right along that Annie was nothing but a child."

"That's it exactly, Mr. Gardner," the social worker concluded. "Annie and Peter are nothing but children. If you'll remember this, you'll have no trouble in understanding them and helping them."

She might have said that they were mental defectives. That she did not was the success of her explanation. She told the relatives about Peter and Annie in terms that were within the range of their experience, using the apparently inexplicable behavior of the Ainsleys as proof of the diagnosis which she advanced — Peter and Annie were nothing but children.

In general, the same methods of interpretation were used both here and in the other instances that have been presented. While the dialogue was devious and prolonged and while what has been reported represents only the climaxes of the various conversations, they all bear testimony to the validity of certain fundamental principles.

If, as with Tony Cavallo, the behavior of the

person who needs to be explained is normal then it is only necessary to show that other people are doing the same thing; if abnormal, as with the Ainsleys, then the plea for understanding should be based upon the special handicaps of their abnormality. One can usually gain a hearing and a sympathetic interest by describing the obstacles with which the individual in trouble must contend, but as with Mr. Reynolds, one must be careful also to give emotions an opportunity to express themselves. Finally, one must never fail to speak in the language of the experience of the man to whom one is talking, always proceeding through the known to the unknown. To observe these axioms of human intercourse is the essence of the art of helping people to understand each other.

CHAPTER X

PLANNING

A man ought to express himself, ought to live his own life, say his own say, before silence comes. The 'say' may be bad — a mere yawp, and silence might be more becoming. But the same argument would make a man dissatisfied with his own nose if it happened to be ugly. It's his nose, and he must content himself. So it's his yawp, and he must let it go. (Walter H. Page in a letter to William Roscoe Thayer, *The Life and Letters of Walter H. Page.*)

THERE is no phase of the art of helping people out of trouble that is more delicate or that cuts closer to the roots of one's philosophy than that which has to do with the development of the plans by which an individual makes his way out of difficulty. As soon as a man appears to hesitate and to be uncertain about his future, there comes the temptation to suggest an appropriate course of action to him. The more obvious the course of action, the greater the temptation. Frequently his friends succumb to it and undertake to tell him what to do, urging and even insisting that he adopt their advice.

To try to help a man in this way is to overlook one of the fundamental human impulses. This is that everybody wants to govern his own life and to make his own decisions. Puzzled, bewildered, and buffeted though a man may be he never loses the urge to self expression. No matter how submissive he may have become to another's suggestions, no matter how prone he may be to turn to some one else for the solution of his problems, when he reaches that which to him is vital he wants to be the arbiter of his own desires.

How can he enter enthusiastically into a plan that is wholly the creation of some one else? He must have had at least a part in its conception. He must feel a sense of ownership in it. Without this there is little hope that the plan will be successfully executed or have anything of permanence about it.

People vary greatly in the ability to devise ways of overcoming their difficulties. Some persons are quick to discover what they should do and need only freedom and opportunity to carry out their decisions. Others find it hard to originate or to develop solutions of their problems. In any event it is by freeing a man so that he can express himself and by stimulating him to do his own thinking that the best plans are developed. We may suggest, we may advise, but only as a subsidiary part of the process by which the indi-

vidual in trouble is working out his own way of
life.

The application of this principle is as various as
are human beings. In one of its aspects it is illustrated by the manner in which George O'Brien
came to arrange for the care of his motherless
baby.

He had fallen in love with Mrs. Ledoux, whose
husband had deserted her, and the young people
— for they were still in their early twenties —
had become parents without marriage. A few
months after the baby's birth, Mrs. Ledoux entered the last stages of consumption. She lived
with her widowed mother and eight brothers and
sisters. For her own comfort and for the protec-
tion of the other members of the family, it was important that she go to a hospital. This she hesitated to do.

The social case worker who had been asked to
help decided to discuss the situation with Mr.
O'Brien, both because she knew that Mrs. Ledoux
would enter the hospital if he wanted her to do so,
and because it was important that some plan be
made for the future of the baby.

"I've been quite anxious to have a talk with
you about Mrs. Ledoux's illness," she said as she

shook hands with Mr. O'Brien. "She's very sick and her mother doesn't seem to realize it. I felt that you ought to know about her condition."

"What did the doctor say?" asked O'Brien who knew that the social worker had consulted Mrs. Ledoux's physician.

"He said that both her lungs were affected. She has scarcely any use of her right lung and her left lung is not much better. I'm afraid that he doesn't feel hopeful. He talked very seriously to me about her. I fear that he doesn't think she is going to get well."

For a moment O'Brien was too shocked to reply.

"I didn't have any idea," he began. "I knew she was sick. I didn't think it was anything like that."

The social worker waited until he had recovered himself. Then she said:

"You know that her home is no place for her in that condition."

"I certainly do," the man agreed. "It makes me sick to go there. I hate even to sit down there."

"We ought to give her every chance, and make her comfortable. Won't you see whether you can persuade her to go to the hospital?"

O'Brien promised to do so, and the social worker continued:

"It's going to be hard for the baby with her mother away. Have you any plan for taking care of the little girl?"

O'Brien seemed to be greatly embarrassed by this turn in the conversation. His face flushed, and it was evident that it was a subject which was not easy for him to discuss. The best way of helping him would probably be to recognize his difficulty:

"I know it's hard for you to speak about this, but I also know how devoted you and Alice are to each other, and I want you to feel that you can talk plainly to me about everything and that I will always understand."

"Yes," O'Brien replied, "I think you would understand. I'm awfully ashamed of having anything like that happen, but I really don't want to do anything until after Alice is in the hospital."

"I think you're right," the social worker agreed. "Of course you will first want to see that Alice is comfortable, but after she goes to the hospital I am afraid that the baby won't get the care she ought to have."

"I've always felt," O'Brien said, "that if anything happened to Alice I would try to do what was right about the baby."

"I'm not surprised to hear you say that. I've respected you ever since I heard about the way you've stuck to Alice and how you helped her after the baby came."

"You're the first one that ever gave me credit for acting white. The whole neighborhood is down on me. They blame me for Alice's being sick."

"That's because they don't understand. You know how the neighbors gossip. If only you could take your little girl away from it all. Do you think your mother could be persuaded to take her?"

"I've never talked to her about it," the man replied. "I don't know how she'd feel about it."

"I know you'd rather have one of your own people take care of the baby, but of course you could always place her with a foster mother. I'm sure I could help you to find one if ever you should want me to."

O'Brien listened thoughtfully.

"As soon as Alice is in the hospital, I will come to see you."

A few days later he told the social worker that

his sister with whom he had decided to make his home had agreed to care for the baby. The plan was carried out, and Mrs. Ledoux had the satisfaction of knowing before she died that the child would be reared by its father, and that its name would be Alice O'Brien.

In all that was essential, the plan for taking care of the child was O'Brien's. The social worker helped him to see that the time for planning had come. She confirmed him in his intention "to do what was right about the baby," but she only suggested. She did not even advise. She was merely the means by which he began to think about what he should do, not an inconsiderable service, to be sure, when it is remembered that most unmarried fathers leave to the mother the responsibility of caring for the child.

Such was the experience of Mrs. Darnell. She had, however, no difficulty in making a plan. What she needed was freedom for carrying it out. She had never been free. She had been so carefully sheltered at home that she had been unprepared for life. At an early age she married a man who soon proved to be unfaithful to her, and after several years of unhappiness she obtained a divorce. The members of her family regarded the whole experience as a reflection upon her ability to direct her own affairs, and they proceeded to manage them for her. They instituted a system of chaperonage and supervision which would have been irksome to a child, but the very man with whom, because he was married, Mrs. Darnell's relatives thought she was safe, became the means of her seduction.

Mrs. Darnell left her home and went to another city where her baby was born. Inasmuch as marriage with the father of the child was impossible, she decided that she would try to make a home for herself and the baby. The only means was a place at service. No one in all her relationship had ever earned a living in this way, and when the members of the family learned about it, they felt that they had been doubly disgraced. Mrs. Darnell's uncle hastened to call upon the social case worker to whom she had turned for advice.

"This must all stop," he announced. "We have everything planned for Edith. She is to come back home where we will take care of her. We'll place the baby in an institution and nobody need know that anything has happened."

Then he asked the social worker to persuade Mrs. Darnell to give up her plan and adopt the one that he suggested. The social worker refused. She pointed out that the family had just witnessed the cost of repression. Why repeat the experiment? Mrs. Darnell now had in her love for the baby a controlling purpose and a reason for living. It was something that would steady and strengthen her. To deprive her of her child and the opportunity to plan her future would be to take away the greatest asset in her life.

The man was unconvinced, but Mrs. Darnell was allowed to carry out her plan. She remained at service until she found employment which enabled her to establish a home for herself and her baby, and there, in less than a year, she entertained the members of her reconciled family. The service of the social worker had been to see that Mrs. Darnell's relatives left her free. Frequently the greatest assistance one can give the person in trouble is to see that other people keep hands off and that he has a chance to work out his own salvation.

It is seldom that a man can act without reference to the ideas of some one else. Often plans must be developed by an interchange of thought between the persons affected. The art of helping may then consist in bringing the interested individuals together so that they may discuss the situation. This was what the social worker did for Peter and Annie Ainsley (described in Chapter IX), when she sat as the chairman of a family council in which a policy and a procedure for helping them were evolved.

Although it is important to leave an individual free to make his own plans, this does not mean that one should blindly endorse every idea that is proposed by the person who comes for advice. The plan must be genuine and must have a reasonable chance of success. What results when these elements are absent is illustrated by the following incident.

A social worker had been endeavoring to aid Harry Wallou, a boy of nineteen years, to discover his vocation. Perhaps because Harry felt that something was expected of him, he said that he would like to be a wireless telegraph operator. It was more a statement at a venture than the expression of a profound desire. It was not a genuine plan. The social worker obtained a job for him in a telegraph office from which, after six months, he was discharged as being utterly incapable of acquiring even the rudiments of wireless telegraphy. The boy's lack of the necessary intelligence and the appropriate educational background could easily have been ascertained before his plan was endorsed. He had not originally suggested it with conviction and it would not have been difficult to show him that the idea was unwise. He might have been spared the additional handicap of the sense of failure which the experience brought him. Only too often a sanguine and enthusiastic personality will embark a man upon plans in which he has no fundamental interest, mistaking his acquiescence for a positive desire. Once the buoyancy and optimism of the helper is removed, the individual slackens his efforts because he has never really made the plan his own.

Sometimes the person in trouble will have a plan which is genuine, but which is unsound. He is so eager to start upon the project that neither persuasion nor advice is enough to make its undesirability evident. Under such circumstances it may be wisest to help him to learn in the only way by which, after all, most people learn, that is, by experience.

A widow with two children was invited by her sister and her brother-in-law to make her home with them. They lived in a city three hundred miles distant. A social case worker learned that the real purpose of the invitation was to use the widow as a servant and that the personality and character of the sister and of her husband were such as to make living with them anything but congenial. She told these things to the widow, but when in spite of this the woman persisted in her wish to carry out her project the social worker helped her to prepare for the journey. Three months later the widow returned to her native city. She had been convinced of her mistake, and was now ready to develop a better plan.

To learn by experience is expensive, and when health and morals are at stake it would seem dangerous to assume the responsibility of making an unwise experiment possible. Would it not be better then to force the individual to adopt the plan that is in his own best interest?

The use of force is always a confession of failure. It implies that one has not at the moment the skill or the knowledge to solve the problem which has been presented, for after all there usually is a solution.

A man who was ill with tuberculosis was unwilling to go to a sanatorium. Yet his carelessness and his failure to take precautions were menacing the health of his children. A social agency which had been supporting the family refused to continue to supply financial assistance so long as he remained at home. The man agreed to enter the sanatorium. After he had been there three months, he returned. When persuasion did not succeed in inducing him to go back, the refusal of support accomplished this purpose. Again he came home, and again the process was repeated. Altogether he was admitted three times to the sanatorium. Three times he returned, and, doubtless, it was only his death at the sanatorium which prevented him from coming back once more. This shows both the effectiveness and the ineffectiveness of force. The man went to the sanatorium, but he had nothing within himself to keep him there; yet, on the other hand, the use of force sent him back and saved his wife and children from contracting his disease.

Sometimes the very fact that a man in such a predicament has a wife and children makes the use of force questionable, for the hardship which the lack of money may cause the family may injure the health of the children more than the presence of the father. The cure is worse than the disease, and there always remains the question, suppose force fails, what then?

Because a person says 'no' to-day does not mean that he will not say 'yes' to-morrow. This was certainly true of John Ellsworth. His mother had died leaving him with seven brothers and sisters, the youngest, a baby. He was only twenty-two years old. His sister Gertrude, was seventeen. She was a stenographer.

"What are you going to do?" asked the social worker.

"Gertrude will give me ten dollars a week," John replied confidently, "and I'm going to take care of the family."

"Have you thought it out thoroughly? It takes a lot of money to clothe and feed so many children and to pay the rent and buy coal."

"I don't care," said John, "that's what I'm going to do."

"Sometime you'll want to marry and have a family of your own. Could you ask a wife to take care of your brothers and sisters? What would you do if Gertrude married and left you to support the whole family? I think you're splendid to have the idea, but don't you think it would be better if the youngest four children were sent to live with some other family? I'll be glad to help you place them."

"There isn't any use talking," John insisted. "I know what I'm going to do and that's keep the children."

The social worker, seeing how determined he was, decided not to press him.

Three or four days later she called again, but did not mention the subject. To do so would only strengthen John in his determination and weaken her influence with him.

A little later John raised the issue.

"You know, I've been thinking that it costs an awful lot of money to keep a family going, and I think the best thing I can do is to put the children away somewhere," and when the social worker offered to help him, he continued, "maybe you could do it better than I could — you just go ahead."

People are hardly ever convinced by argument. When a man has positive opinions, it is seldom wise to oppose him. It is vastly better to wait until more opportunity for thought or the logic of events convinces him. Then, when he arrives at a decision, the plan is his own.

The more difficult the plan is of execution, the more vital to the individual in trouble does the sense of personal identity with it become. It was this which caused a social case worker to wait a year and a half for a family to decide upon a course of action, which during all this time she felt was necessary to their happiness. Husband and wife had begun to jar each other's nerves. With rest and recuperation for the woman and a stay in a sanatorium for the man, the physical basis of their oversensitiveness to each other might be removed. But in order to accomplish this it would be necessary to break up the home and place the children temporarily with some private family. This would be a difficult step for the parents to take. The social worker knew that if she persuaded them to do it they would not be nearly so likely to hold to their decision as if they arrived at it of their own accord. Therefore, she suggested the plan and then waited until at last they came to see that it was the only possible solution of their difficulties.

The more one works with people the more one realizes that the way of freedom is the only sure road to success. The plan that carries through is the plan that is a man's own. Suggest it to him, perhaps, but only as a thought for him to digest and to make a part of himself. Offer him the stimulation that comes from a meeting of minds,

from the action and reaction of ideas, from the
thinking out aloud with some one who understands; edit, perhaps criticize, but let the author-
ship remain with him. It is both his right and
the way of his salvation.

CHAPTER XI

THE CULTIVATION OF RESPONSIBILITY

The greatest mentality in the sea has been repeatedly derived from the continents, first in the fishes, then in the reptiles, and lastly in the mammals, and they have adapted themselves to the sea because of the ease with which they can there prey upon the less alert and intelligent. Such adapted stocks in the course of geologic time grow larger and larger, as, for instance, the whales of today. Out of them, however, comes no higher mentality. They represent an adaptation in the wrong direction, that is, to an easier life, for the highest organisms with the greatest mentality have been developed only on the land where the struggle for existence is fiercest because of the constant necessity of adaptation to an environment subject to intense changes. Organic supremacy is attained only through constant vigilance. (CHARLES SCHUCHERT, *The Evolution of the Earth and its Inhabitants*, chap. II, "The Earth's Changing Surface and Climate during Geologic Time.")

AT the opposite pole of human nature from man's desire to think and act for himself is his tendency to thrust upon others the solution of his problems. In its insidious way this inclination to escape responsibility is as strong as his will to achieve his own salvation. It appears at every stage of life, from childhood to age, and, while it varies in intensity in different people, it is absent from no one.

Weakness and inability are its special opportunity. The strong man obviously is able to take care of himself, and is expected to do so. There is no excuse for him to transfer his responsibilities, and therefore less temptation for him to do so, but where there is weakness the opposite prevails. Then the need of help is recognized and the person in trouble by reason of his own insufficiency can hope that his fellows will carry his burdens. Many things are done for the sick which in health they would do for themselves. Children being unable to cope with all the vicissitudes of life unaided are spared responsibilities which in later years they must assume. The loss of a job may force a man to accept assistance in meeting his financial obligations, and there are many other circumstances in which people are relieved of tasks which ordinarily they would be expected to assume.

Unless help of this kind is extended with understanding and foresight, it may become like the morphine which, having been administered out of the necessity for deadening pain, proves to be the means of forming in the patient an addiction to opiates. Once a man has enjoyed the luxury of having had his responsibilities carried by some one else, he finds the temptation to continue the period of weakness exceedingly difficult to resist.

Every one has moments when he does not feel

like exerting himself, and when he would willingly yield to this disinclination even though at the expense of other people. All that we need at such a time is a sufficient excuse. We tell ourselves that the hot weather is especially hard for us to bear; or it may be that we still feel the effects of the influenza; or perhaps we are not qualified by experience for the undertaking; or, as a last resort, we just do not feel equal to it. If we can prove this to ourselves we feel that we can preserve our self-respect; and if we can lead others to believe us we can induce them to do our work for us.

This tendency which all of us occasionally experience may become greatly accentuated in any one who frequently or over a long period of time has received help from others. He finds effort more and more difficult and dependence easier and easier, until at last his energies seem to suffer a kind of atrophy and he becomes a parasite upon his friends and a handicap to all with whom he is associated.

One way of treating a person thus affected and of preventing his deterioration is to place responsibility upon him and to expect accomplishment of him. The doing of this involves more an attitude of mind than a definite procedure, a point of view that will be found to be more strongly developed in some persons than in others. Is it not true that there is a vast variation in the amount of effort which different people draw from us? As between two men, equally friendly, equally interested in us, we will be more careful to present accomplishment to one than to the other, more punctilious in the keeping of appointments, more precise in the making of statements, more effective in every way. The reason for this is that we feel that the one expects more of us than does the other. The same fact holds good of our attitude toward those whom we are helping out of trouble. We can make our assistance stimulating or we can make it enervating in proportion as we look for strength or invite weakness. There is nothing more difficult in the art of helping than this, for one must maintain a nice balance between doing everything and doing nothing, varying the weight of responsibility according to the strength of the individual who is being helped. This calls for the most intimate knowledge of the person in difficulty, and even then, one is frequently at a loss to know how much or how little of achievement should be expected of him.

Perhaps the simplest illustration of this is provided by the experience of a father and his daughter, who, one winter's day, were climbing a hill down which they had coasted. The snow was covered with a crust. Through this the man occasionally broke and therefore found the ascent easier than did the girl, a child of about five years, who, as they came to the steep rise that defended the top, began to be in difficulty. Her feet slipped from under her. She fell. She slid back, and it seemed almost as if she would be unable to complete the climb. The father was greatly tempted to put forth his hand and pull the child out of trouble. Instead, he encouraged her to continue the struggle. Walking now beside her, now half a pace ahead, he tried to make a game of it, laughing whenever the child fell, but with her, not at her, and cheering her on to greater effort, until at length the hill was conquered. Thereafter, with the experience and assurance of her first success the little girl repeated the victory with increasing ease. The mastery of the ascent strengthened her for the next attempt. Had not this achievement been expected of her she would have been by just that much retarded in the development of self-confidence. At the same time, however, that her father was placing the responsibility of making the climb upon her he was helping her to accomplish it. He gave her the assistance of his encouragement and he aided her by pulling the sled up the hill. Had she been older and stronger, they would have pulled the sled together, or perhaps have taken turns, but the father recognized what was possible and what was not possible, and asked of her only that which she could perform.

This recognition of the possible and the impossible is admittedly the crux of the problem of placing responsibility, a problem that cannot be solved by rule, but can be dealt with only on the basis of one's understanding of the person whom he is helping. Generally speaking, parents in comfortable circumstances are likely to underestimate rather than to overestimate the capacity of their children. Necessity compels the poor to expect self-reliance of their sons and daughters, but their wealthier neighbors have not this advantage. It is not unusual for boys and girls of families in comfortable circumstances to enter the first year of school without being able to dress themselves, or even to lace their shoes, while the overanxiety of parents and the availability of motor-cars prevents many a child of eight or nine years of age from learning to go to school alone.

Occasionally one finds instances of exactly the reverse of this, parents who expect too much too quickly. This often causes the children to feel that their elders have no sympathy for them and no understanding of them. Responsibility and self-dependence should be cultivated gradually, as was done by the parents of a seven-year-old girl in accustoming her to take herself to and from school.

The child lived where electric cars and automobiles passed continually, and the possibility of such an accident as every city mother dreads was always present. On leaving the electric car to walk to the school she was obliged to cross the street with its double tracks, and then, at the end of a block, a thoroughfare where the motor traffic was exceptionally heavy. The parents began by accustoming their daughter to the passage of the street on which their home stood. At first the mother crossed with the child, emphasizing, by example, the importance of watching for electric cars and automobiles, and of waiting for lulls in traffic. After a time she went only so far as the curb, leaving the little girl to complete the remainder of the journey alone. The next step was to watch from the window until her daughter waved to her from the other side.

While the child was learning this lesson — and the home of a playmate across the way provided frequent occasion for it — one or the other of the parents took her to school. As soon as she had acquired the necessary skill and confidence, they began to reduce the distance which they accompanied her at the school end of her journey, first stopping to watch her cross the automobile thoroughfare; then going only to the farther side of the street with the double car tracks, and at last discharging her from their tutelage by remaining on the electric car while she stepped off by herself. Could any procedure be more simple? Yet, for lack of such elementary processes as these, children are sheltered beyond the years when they should be relying upon themselves.

Nor is it only children who are unwisely protected in this way. The same mistake is frequently made by those who undertake to help people of foreign birth to adjust themselves to American life. Thus, a young woman who had entered training for social work devoted several hours each week for a number of months to taking a woman of immigrant stock to a dispensary. The trip involved a change of cars which apparently the woman did not feel able to manage. Later, an experienced social case worker became acquainted with the woman. She explained that she would accompany her to the dispensary once more so that she could observe the way, but that she was too busy to undertake more than this one trip. The next expedition the woman made alone, and thereafter she continued to attend the dispensary without a companion.

Often it is the subtle appeal to the pride of having some one consult us that prevents us from expecting accomplishment of the individual who seeks our help. There is nothing quite so flattering as to be asked to give advice. When a man comes to us in trouble we find it hard to resist telling him what, if we were in his place, we should do, and if he is at all inclined to be dependent upon others we are likely to assume the responsibility for most of his decisions, gradually depriving him of his self-reliance.

This was the way in which the spirit of dependence had been developed in Henry Norton. His parents had died before he had reached ten years of age, and an aunt had become his guardian. She was a woman of strong personality, and this, together with her pity for her orphaned, and to her mind, therefore, helpless nephew, caused her to take the initiative in all decisions. The boy learned to turn to her for the solution of his every problem. He became more and more dependent upon her, a dependence of which apparently he was quite unconscious until her death in a railroad accident.

Without her he seemed to be unable to direct his life, and in his dilemma he turned eagerly to the social case worker who had met him in the course of her work among the survivors of the disaster. Where should he live? What would she suggest? The social worker recognizing his difficulty felt that to throw him immediately upon his own resources would be to send him to a dependence upon the first sympathetic person whom he might meet. On the other hand, to tell him what to do would be but to continue him in a habit which was already too strong. She decided upon a compromise.

"Well, what is there that you can do?" she asked. "Have you any place at all where you could live?"

"My things are at the apartment, but I couldn't live there alone, could I?"

"Would you want to?"

"It would be lonely. What do you think I ought to do?"

"How do the students at the university find rooms?" This question was designed to open the way for a new plan.

"There is a registry of houses at the Dean's office, and sometimes they answer advertisements in the newspapers."

The social worker purposely offered no suggestion, and the young man added, "I suppose I could go to see the Dean."

Having visited a number of possible living places, he returned. He wanted the social worker to make a choice for him. She questioned him about the advantages and disadvantages of each house, but when he asked her where she would go, if she were in his place, she put the responsibility upon him. "You're the only person who can decide where you want to live," she told him.

Finally, he made the choice, uncertainly, and tentatively, but nevertheless his own. It was a wise selection, and the social worker added to his assurance by telling him so.

Almost immediately thereafter Norton was obliged to make up his mind about whether he should return to the university for a year of post-graduate study, or whether he should enter the field of advertising where an opportunity had been opened to him. Again, he turned to the social worker, and again she helped him by the indirect method of questioning instead of by telling him what to do. She paralleled advantages and disadvantages for him, but having done this she once more placed the decision upon his shoulders.

The man with whom Norton was now making his home perceived the young man's problem and supplemented the work of developing his spirit of self-reliance. The following comment was typical of the way in which this friend threw Norton back upon his own resources.

"The engine is stalled and I think I'll ask her to crank it," Norton had said by way of explaining that he was discouraged and was going to the social worker for inspiration.

"Wouldn't she prefer having you use a self-starter?" was the man's reply.

Norton had not thought of this. He decided to be his own inspiration. The process was repeated again and again, for once a person has contracted the habit of depending upon others for advice, he is not likely to break himself of it in a week, nor yet in a month.

This is not to imply that to give advice, and, when possible, to provide inspiration is not a legitimate and important form of helpfulness. To establish a principle of never doing this would be as unwise as always to supply it whenever it was asked. There is, however, a place beyond which one cannot go. This is where one finds the burden of decisions resting upon himself instead of — where it belongs — upon the person who is striving to make a better adjustment to life.

Sickness and physical handicap are perhaps the most difficult circumstances in which to tell whether or not — and to what extent — one should carry the responsibility of the individual in trouble. It is not so much in the acute illnesses that this question arises, for the man who is in the midst of one of these attacks obviously is capable of no exertion other than that involved in the will to recover. It is rather during convalescence, in chronic handicaps, or in minor indispositions that the issue develops.

In such situations the patient frequently believes that he is unable to undertake any of the usual activities of life and is in constant fear of what may happen to him if he attempts them. This caution is well founded. Any one whose vitality has been drained by disease or who has suffered the results of too early a return to work knows how justifiable and significant is the inclination to continue the period of incapacity. During illness the patient's willingness to abandon his ordinary tasks is often the measure of his chances of recovery; but not always. Sometimes the feeling of incapacity and the fear of effort may prevent a man from realizing that he is no longer ill or from appreciating that even in the presence of certain kinds of handicap a useful and interesting life can be lived. How many persons with weak hearts have betaken themselves to an unhappy invalidism despite the experience of those who in the same condition have been able to fulfill the ordinary demands of business. The belief that an individual who has had tuberculosis is stopped from any but that elusive occupation known as light outdoor work has become so firmly embedded in the minds of people that a physician will often have the greatest difficulty in convincing his patient that he can work eight hours a day in a great variety of employments.

The tendency here and in like situations is toward a construing of the physician's diagnosis of disease in terms of an abandonment of effort, when what he intends is a more reasoned and a more intelligent activity.

This tendency is encouraged by the attitude of the friends of the convalescent or handicapped person. Out of a mistaken chivalry and in their desire to help they frequently confirm him in the feeling that he is not equal to the ordinary exigencies of life. This was what made a beggar of Harold Griffin. At the end of his last year in grammar school he met with an accident which necessitated the amputation of one of his legs. On regaining his strength he decided to go to work; but instead of aiding him to realize his plan, those from whom he sought employment expressed their sympathy by offering him money, until at length the boy decided that people did not expect him to support himself, and for four years he relied upon this kind of misdirected generosity.

Illness can become a habit. The longer a person is led to think of himself as an invalid the greater is the temptation to continue in this state of mind. He becomes confirmed in the feeling that he is too sick to do things for himself and he becomes willing that others should carry his burdens.

Complicating the problem of dealing with people who have acquired this habit is the fact that often one cannot tell whether the illness is real or imagined. Sometimes this unwillingness once more to assume the responsibilities of life is entirely unconscious. The person who has been sick and then convalescent over a number of months has during this time been removed from the struggle for existence. He has been able to think and to plan without translating his thoughts and his plans into action. Except for the recovery of his health he is likely to have no fixed purpose and his attention and his interests scatter. He dreams over the things he would like to do, but does not point them in any one direction. He talks about working but he does not realize that he has lost the habit of effort and that there has been insidiously developing within him a disinclination to action.

Even under such circumstances it is possible to throw responsibility upon an individual. This may be seen in the manner in which a social case worker dealt with a man who, after having had influenza, complained of not being well enough to return to his job. So many people are not strong enough to work for months after their apparent recovery from this disease that the social worker was puzzled about what to do. Finally, after consultation with a physician and with the man's former employer, she devised a scheme of graduated employment, beginning with three hours a day. The man could not deny his ability to work for so brief a period. After he had become accustomed to this schedule, it was lengthened, until at last he was busy eight hours out of twenty-four.

What added to the difficulty of this man's problem was the presence of financial as well as physical disability. During the period that his illness had prevented him from working he had been dependent for his living upon money which had been supplied to him by the social worker. It was therefore all the harder for him to overcome the temptation to find in his weakness an excuse for avoiding effort. For financial assistance, while frequently required by the person in trouble, is so obvious and so tangible a way of having his burdens carried by others that unless administered with the utmost wisdom it may cause a man to abandon his initiative and the exercise of his energies.

Most people still need the incentive to accomplishment that springs from economic necessity and material wants. How few of us if suddenly supplied with money enough to provide for these things would continue to work with the same concentration. Unless already in the grip of some dynamic interest we would probably follow the example of Jacob Wesley.

Wesley had completed a course in mechanical engineering and was about to start upon his career when he received a legacy involving an annual income of two thousand dollars. This took from work its imperative immediacy and he found one good reason after another for postponing action. First, it was a trip to Europe to complete his education, then it was a visit to some relatives, and after this it was the difficulty of finding just the right sort of an opening. When at last he took a job he could not forget that he was not obliged to work. This prevented him from developing an interest in his occupation and he soon left it. After a period of idleness he obtained another job which after a brief trial he abandoned. He drifted about here and there without cultivating his abilities.

Then an industrial depression took his income

from him. His necessity might now quite possibly have been the making of him had not an aunt interfered. She felt so sorry for him that she gave him money upon which to live while seeking work. It was only a few hundred dollars, but it made a virtue of procrastination. When the money had been spent, Wesley did not find it difficult to suggest that he required a little more time to settle his affairs. Soon his aunt had grown as accustomed to giving as he to asking, and the opportunity to make a man of himself had passed.

Essentially there is no difference between the loss in initiative and the sense of responsibility which Wesley suffered and the dependence and beggary brought about in the boy who, on seeking a job after the amputation of his leg, received gifts of money instead of employment. The boy was seduced by dimes and quarters and Wesley by checks and banknotes, but the result was the same.

Dependence induced in this way is more complete and more demoralizing than that occasioned by any other form of reliance upon others. This is because money is vastly more than a medium of exchange. It is the symbol and the trophy of man's struggle for existence. It is the measure of his ability to provide for himself and his family. The instinct of self-preservation has made it the first, the most primitive, and the most widely recognized criterion of success — witness the satisfaction with which a wage-earner will remark as he looks back over the years, "I've always been able to support my family," or the manner in which a worker, now come upon hard times, will exclaim by way of describing past achievements, "Those were the days when I had money in my pocket."

Correspondingly great is the humiliation of the man who is obliged to confess his failure to meet this age-old test of manhood by taking as a gift the livelihood that other men are earning for themselves. It matters not whether the amount of money involved be great or small. His self-respect has been invaded. He has been obliged to yield his independence, and in its place there often comes a feeling of futility and of inferiority. He ceases trying to do things for himself and weakly allows others to carry his burdens.

When financial difficulties appear as part of a man's trouble, every possible measure should be taken to make it unnecessary for him to accept money as a gift. Perhaps he can be aided to find more remunerative employment. Perhaps a wiser household management will fit his present resources to his needs. Perhaps he can call still further upon his credit. Every conceivable resource which a man may have should be developed in the hope that by capitalizing past or future productivity he may succeed in meeting the crisis in his finances.

If his assets are not sufficient to his necessity and financial assistance is inevitable, then money should be given to him in such a way as to stimulate his sense of responsibility. This can be done through a careful selection of the source from which help comes to him. It should, if possible, suggest the idea of reciprocity. Thus, assistance from a member of the same family or from a friend, for whom in a similar situation he might conceivably perform a similar service, is better than aid from a stranger or from some one whose financial status is such as to render remote the possibility of his needing help. Aid from an employer contains the element of reciprocity, for there is, on the one hand, a growing public opinion that the employee contributes to industry more than the amount of his wages, and, on the other, the hope of the employee that in the future he may be able to make return in more effective work. Money received from the union or the church or the lodge to which an individual belongs has the virtue of appearing as a prerogative of his membership. On previous occasions his dues or his contributions may have gone to aid others. Now it is his turn. Perhaps later on he will once more be able to help some fellow member.

What the conception of reciprocity may do to foster the individual's sense of responsibility can be supplemented by expecting accomplishment of him in return for the money he receives. Financial assistance should always be supplied as part of a definite plan toward the execution of which the person in trouble must work. If he is sick, the goal may be his restoration to health. If he is out of work, it may be employment. If the individual in need of assistance is a mother, then the plan may center about the education of her children. The more definite the undertaking and the greater the emphasis upon what the person who is receiving help must do, the better are the chances of safeguarding his initiative and his self-respect.

Whenever the gift of money is necessary, this is the spirit in which it should be given, the same spirit in which every approach to people in trouble should be made, whether the assistance be financial or inspirational. Only thus can one prevent what one does for a man from becoming a temptation to him to allow his burden to be carried by others. To insist that he do his own thinking and that he act for himself is indispensable to his rehabilitation. It is the best way of showing respect for his ability and confidence in him, and this in turn has the effect of quickening his own confidence in himself. What we expect of an individual determines in large measure what he does. Give him responsibility, and he will develop in self-reliance and self-dependence.

CHAPTER XII

MOTIVATION

I know a very pretty instance of a little girl of whom her father was very fond, who once when he was in a melancholy fit, and had gone to bed, persuaded him to rise in good humor by saying, "My dear papa, please to get up, and let me help you on with your clothes, that I may learn to do it when you are an old man." (JAMES BOSWELL, in the *Life of Samuel Johnson*.)

A CERTAIN elderly gentleman was discovered by his relatives to be living a hermit's life on the top floor of a cheap and wretched rooming house. He was a university graduate, a person of taste and refinement, who had traveled widely and had been accustomed to wealth. Domestic troubles had left him without a home and he had drifted hither and thither as circumstance directed, until at last he had reached his present miserable quarters.

Here for three winters he had occupied two rooms which were without means of heating. He had furnished them — if it could be said that they were furnished — with the odds and ends that remained from the days when he had had a house of his own. The bed clothing consisted of a thin and ragged quilt. There were neither rugs nor carpet on the floor, and despite his retention of habits of personal neatness, there was dust and dirt everywhere, even vermin.

Gradually he had become isolated from intercourse with his kind. He went out less and less, and began to depend for his food upon sandwiches and fruit which a neighbor's boy brought to him. The paper bags in which his lunches had been carried formed a considerable part of the rubbish with which his room was littered. He was beset with aches and pains of many sorts, chiefly the result of this irregular way of living, and he was wretchedly unhappy. He spent the hours worrying about his present and his future, and regretting his past.

A social worker was asked to help him to move to an environment where he would be comfortable and where he would find friends, but when it came to the point, the old gentleman could not make up his mind to go. He was well acquainted with the facts of his situation. He knew what it would mean to pass another winter in unheated rooms. He was miserable in his loneliness and in the barrenness and the inconvenience of his quarters. He had none of the attachment for them that age frequently has for its home. He wanted to escape from the wretchedness of his present condition, but his desire to move was not strong enough to decide him in favor of a change.

It was to the quickening of this desire that the social worker addressed himself. Having discovered a possible boarding-house, he suggested that the old man go with him to inspect it, for there is nothing more effective in bringing an individual to a decision than the presentation of a concrete proposition which must be either accepted or refused.

The social worker set forth the arguments in favor of the new living place: its location in a suburb which was within a single fare by electric car of the center of the city, so that visits to town would be easy and cheap; the beauty of its surroundings, especially as contrasted with the neighborhood in which the old gentleman was now living; the convenience of the room that was to be had for rent, and the charming view from its windows; the advantage of being able to eat and sleep under the same roof, the regular living which this would make possible, and the influence it would have in restoring his health; the quietness of the place — there would be only three or four other boarders; and the pleasant character of the woman in charge, a registered nurse who would be able to take care of him when he was not feeling well. Why not at least go to look at the house?

The old gentleman feared that it was beyond his means. He was assured that the allowance which he received from his relatives would amply provide for this. Suppose that the allowance should stop? In reply he was told that his relatives had pledged themselves to his support, and, should by any chance the unforeseen occur, the social worker would see to it that he did not suffer thereby.

Then the social worker described how worried about him his niece was, and how happy it would make her to know that he was comfortable and well. The man's eyes filled with tears, but he looked at the furniture about the room and felt that he could not move. What was he to do with it all? It was like a rope around his neck.

The social worker promised to undertake the moving. He would bring an assistant and the old gentleman could sit in a chair and watch while they disposed of things as he desired. What he did not want to keep could be sold. He could move to his new home without any of the worry that having these possessions gave him.

And what a terrible thing it was for a man of his tastes and his education to be living in this way. He should be in the sort of surroundings to which he had been accustomed, not in these dismal quarters.

Such were the suggestions which the social worker advanced to develop within the old gentleman the desire to move to a better environment. Back and forth over this ground the conversation went, the suggestions being introduced from different angles. Finally, after a discussion of more than two hours, the man promised to think over it by himself that night. The next day he called at the office of the social worker and said that he had decided to move.

Perhaps the inertia of the old gentleman — he said of himself that once he was settled in a place he was likely to stay — was unusual, but it serves to emphasize a fundamental fact in human nature. People may be convinced intellectually of the importance of a given course of action, yet they may not rally the energy necessary to carry it through. The truth of this, as applied to the breaking of habits, almost everybody will recognize. Moderation in eating and in the selection of proper foods is universally agreed to be essential, yet hosts of men and women suffer from various afflictions and inconveniences because, while they realize that they ought to control their diet, they cannot bring themselves to do so. Those who are victims of the habit of retiring late find themselves, day after day, less effective than they might be, but although they want more sleep and realize the importance of this, they seem to be unable to go to bed at an appropriate hour. A knowledge of the facts, an appreciation of the relation between habits such as these and personal inefficiency is seldom alone enough to enable an individual to modify his manner of life. To overcome his trouble he must want to be free of it more than he desires to indulge himself. Other things being equal, if his wish to enter upon a new régime is strong enough he will change.

One way of aiding a man in such a situation is to reinforce his desire with other desires, to strengthen the influence of one motive by appealing to supporting motives. It was this which caused Tom Haverstraw to go to a sanitarium after he had become so suspicious of hospitals and other institutions that he had run away from several in which he had been staying. Tom was suffering from a form of hysteria which had twisted his arm and neck from their natural positions. Among the things prescribed for his cure was a regularized life and an environment in which he would find quiet and security. This he could not obtain at home; yet while he wanted to recover, he could not bring himself to leave his parents.

One day he happened to complain about insomnia.

"If I could only sleep," he sighed.

"When I can't sleep," said the social case worker, "I take a vacation and go to the country and I soon find that I can sleep." She then described the restfulness of the fields and woods and the quiet of the night.

"My, I wish I could go somewhere like that," the boy exclaimed.

"You can," the social worker assured him, and told him about a sanitarium situated in beautiful country where he could find the very peace and repose he was seeking. The boy decided to go. The wish to recover the use of his neck and arms was not enough to cause him to want to leave home, but as soon as the hope of recovering from insomnia was added to this wish he was ready to try the experiment.

When he arrived at the institution, the superintendent used another motive as a means of strengthening his determination to regain his health. A few steps away two boys were shouting and running about apparently with every muscle and nerve under their command.

"Jim, Harry," the superintendent called. "Come here a minute, please."

The boys came up with leaps and skips.

"Boys," asked the superintendent, "were you as badly off as Tom, here, when you came to us?"

"Oh, we were much worse," they replied.

"So you see, Tom," said the superintendent, "you can get well if you want to. If you really want to get well you will."

This was both an assurance and a challenge. The superintendent was using the age-old suggestion that "all may do what has by man been done." It was both a means of instilling confidence in the boy, and an appeal to the spirit of competition.

A typical use of this latter motive was that made by a social case worker in encouraging Mrs. Dorello to fix up her home. The house was in a most dilapidated state. It had not been papered for eight years. What paper was left on the walls was hanging in shreds. The paint was smudged with the grime of countless dirty fingers, but the landlord having no confidence in the capacity of the family for taking care of his property refused to make any improvements. The mattresses were filthy and there were only two sheets that even approached serviceability.

The social worker had tried to help Mrs. Dorello to find a better house, but the shortage of dwellings was so great that this was impossible. Knowing that Mrs. Dorello knew what earnest efforts had been made to secure a better home for the family the social worker suggested that she try to make the best of the one she had. Mr. Dorello was out of the city. Why not surprise him and welcome him back to a spick and span home? Why not try to do over everything before he should return? Partly it was the fun of surprising her husband and partly the spirit of competing against time which stimulated Mrs. Dorello's energy. She tore the remaining paper from the walls and whitewashed them. She painted the woodwork, washed the mattresses, obtained new sheets, and did many other things, so that when her husband returned he found a new home awaiting him.

To make a game of a task is one of the easiest ways of accomplishing it. Parents, in particular, appreciate this, as is instanced by such familiar expedients in the lives of children as the race to get dressed in the morning, or the finishing of this or that before the mother or the father comes home. Competition against space, or time, or one's self, or somebody else, frequently, if not always, underlies the idea of the game. It is an exceedingly useful motive if not practiced to excess, and if the competition most often called into practice is competition against one's self.

With some people, the spirit of competition really becomes one of combativeness. The surest way to rouse their energies to is oppose them, and sometimes the best method of stimulating them to carry out what they have undertaken is to advocate an opposite course.

A delightful illustration of this is set forth by Boswell in his famous description of how he persuaded Dr. Johnson to dine with John Wilkes to whom the doctor was violently opposed, Wilkes being a strong Whig, while Johnson, of course, was a vehement Tory. "Two men more different could perhaps not be selected out of all mankind," says Boswell. "They had even attacked one

another with some asperity in their writings."
Indeed, when Boswell suggested to Mr. Edward
Dilly that he invite Dr. Johnson to his house to
dine with Mr. Wilkes, Mr. Dilly exclaimed:

"What! with Mr. Wilkes? Not for the world.
Dr. Johnson would never forgive me."

Boswell, however, undertook to arrange the
meeting.

"Notwithstanding the high veneration which I
entertained for Dr. Johnson, I was sensible that
he was sometimes a little actuated by the spirit of
contradiction, and by means of that I hoped that
I should gain my point. I was persuaded that if
I had come upon him with a direct proposal, 'Sir,
will you dine in company with Jack Wilkes' he
would have flown into a passion, and would
probably have answered, 'Dine with Jack Wilkes,
Sir! I'd as soon dine with Jack Ketch.' I, therefore, while we were sitting quietly by ourselves at
his house in an evening, took occasion to open
my plan thus: — 'Mr. Dilly, Sir, sends his re-
spectful compliments to you, and would be happy
if you would do him the honor to dine with him
on Wednesday next along with me, as I must soon
go to Scotland.' Johnson. 'Sir, I am obliged to
Mr. Dilly. I will wait upon him — ' Boswell

'Provided, Sir, I suppose, that the company which he is to have, is agreeable to you.' Johnson. 'What do you mean, Sir? What do you take me for? Do you think I am so ignorant of the world, as to imagine that I am to prescribe to a gentleman what company he is to have at his table?' Boswell. 'I beg your pardon, Sir, for wishing to prevent you from meeting people whom you might not like. Perhaps he may have some of what he calls his patriotick friends with him.' Johnson. 'Well, Sir, and what then? What care I for his patriotick friends? Poh!' Boswell. 'I should not be surprised to find Jack Wilkes there.' Johnson. 'And if Jack Wilkes should be there, what is that to me, Sir? My dear friend, let me have no more of this. I am sorry to be angry with you; but really it is treating me strangely to talk to me as if I could not meet any company whatever occasionally.' Boswell. 'Pray forgive me, Sir: I meant well. But you shall meet whoever comes, for me.' Thus I secured him, and told Dilly that he would find him very well pleased to be one of his guests on the day appointed."

Boswell's method of motivating Dr. Johnson was not unlike the means used to induce a man suffering from tuberculosis to enter a sanatorium.

Argument and persuasion had been tried without any effect. Although at bottom the man knew that he ought to go his determination to stay where he was increased with each suggestion to the contrary. Finally the social worker said to him:

"I've tried my best to induce you to go to the sanatorium. But since you will not do so, I'm not going to try any longer. We'll do the best we can to make you comfortable at home and we'll not mention the sanatorium any more."

When the man found himself with nothing to oppose he became less certain about his desire to continue in the city, and very shortly he began to make plans for going away for treatment. After the social case worker had yielded, the man could not help feeling, now that he had succeeded in having his way, a little ashamed of his perverseness.

Pride, and its corollary shame, are among the strongest motives to which one can appeal.

"Why, you're a slacker, aren't you?" said a social case worker to a boy as he entered her office one morning during the war, coughing heavily.

The boy straightened up and took a step forward almost as if he were about to strike her.

"What do you mean?" he asked.

"If you let that cough run on, the army won't accept you when your turn comes," was the reply.

"When can I go to the doctor?" was the boy's almost instant response. He stopped smoking, and recovered from his cough. The boy had wanted to be rid of his cough, but not until his pride had been touched at its most sensitive point, his courage, and at a time when courage was at a premium, was he willing to make the sacrifice upon which his recovery was contingent.

"Don't let the neighbors see you move anything into the house that isn't in first-class condition," urged the social worker upon Mrs. Dorello when at last another home had been found. "You are going into a new neighborhood. Don't let them think that you own anything that is dirty."

Mr. and Mrs. Dorello rose immediately to this suggestion. They washed the beds and painted them; they gilded the frames of their pictures; repaired furniture; scoured the pots and pans; and disposed of all the odds and ends that were not worth saving; and thus were able to make a fresh start in keeping house.

A similar appeal to pride and shame was that

made to a man who, while his wife was ill in a hospital, asked:

"What about my wife? Must I still stay with that woman?"

"Would you go and leave her now that she's sick?" said the social worker.

"I don't like her and I don't want to stay with her."

"Does it mean nothing to you that she is the mother of all your children?" was the reply. "Think what she has endured to bring them into the world and what it has meant to her to take care of them. You wouldn't want people to say, 'There goes Hansen. Look at the kind of man he is. He just walked off and left his wife and family.'"

A simple appeal of this sort to a man's pride is obviously not alone enough to solve a problem of maladjustment between husband and wife. There were many other things that needed to be done, but the use of this motive was not without its effect, as was also a reference to the welfare of his children.

"If you and your wife quarrel, your children can't be happy. You must find a way to be happy yourself if you want to have a happy home."

The part which the desire for the welfare of others may play in influencing people is illustrated by the story of Mr. and Mrs. Henshaw.

Mr. Henshaw had been a patient in the Hudson Tuberculosis Hospital. It became necessary to close the ward in which he was staying, and preparations for his transfer to another institution were made. He, however, decided to return to his home. As he was in an advanced stage of the disease, this plan would have jeopardized the health of the family. The social worker and the doctors who had been helping Mr. Henshaw did their best to persuade him to enter the other hospital. Finally, when he refused, they threatened to invoke the aid of the law permitting the compulsory removal of tuberculous patients from their homes. Mr. Henshaw responded by falling into a tremendous fury and leaving the ward. When the social worker called at his home, he refused her admission. Both he and his wife were enraged. Those who knew Mr. and Mrs. Henshaw said that they were stubborn, impossible people.

Another social case worker then undertook to change the attitude of Mr. and Mrs. Henshaw and to induce Mr. Henshaw to enter a sanatorium.

Mrs. Henshaw received her.

"How are things going?" the visitor asked.

The only response was a shrug of the shoulders.

"Not very well?" suggested the social worker.

"No; how could they go well?" replied Mrs. Henshaw in a moody and aggrieved tone of voice. "My husband is no better, the damp weather has a depressing effect upon him. He has been in bed most of the week."

"What are you planning to do for him?"

"He is to stay at home," replied Mrs. Henshaw. "I know that I can take care of him." She then burst into a torrent of feeling. "He has been in the Hudson Hospital all winter and is no better. The doctors have done him no good. When he wanted to leave, they threatened him with the law. If he could have gone to Mount Huron last summer as I wanted, he would be all right now. It is the one place away from home where he would be happy. I don't see why you won't send him there."

"Do you believe he has tuberculosis?"

"I know he has," admitted Mrs. Henshaw.

She had never been willing to acknowledge this before. It was for this reason that the social case worker had asked the question. Had she told

Mrs. Henshaw that her husband had tuberculosis, the statement would probably have been hotly contradicted. By this method of approach the social worker had avoided an issue.

"There is no sanatorium at Mount Huron," she now explained, "and there is no other place there where a person with consumption can go."

"Well, if he can't go to Mount Huron," returned Mrs. Henshaw, "he won't go to the Mercy Hospital" — this being the institution to which the doctors had tried to induce Mr. Henshaw to go.

Having learned Mrs. Henshaw's plan and having by inference at least obtained from her the recognition of its impossibility, the social worker began to prepare the way for inducing Mrs. Henshaw to encourage her husband to enter an institution.

"What about the children?" she began. "Are you going to risk exposing them to tuberculosis? You wouldn't expose them to measles or scarlet fever, and tuberculosis is a much more dangerous disease."

"That's not true," exclaimed Mrs. Henshaw, raising her voice. "He's no more a danger than the other patients, and the hospital discharged them without asking any questions."

Evidently this was not a good start. With some women the argument of the welfare of their children is unanswerable. With others, the welfare of the husband comes first. Mrs. Henshaw had in spirit suffered all the pain and discomfort that Mr. Henshaw had experienced.

"Wouldn't you like your husband to get away from the city before the hot weather?" was the next suggestion. "He now has a middle room with very little air, and he might be in a place where he would not feel the heat so much. Wouldn't you like something of that sort for him?"

"Yes, I would," Mrs. Henshaw admitted.

"Do you think he would consider the Lakeview Sanatorium?" — a pleasant institution near the country which would be favorably known to Mrs. Henshaw. To have suggested the Mercy Hospital would have been merely to arouse old antagonisms, and by asking Mrs. Henshaw's advice in this way the social worker was in a sense making her a partner in the effort to persuade Mr. Henshaw.

"I'll talk to him about it," Mrs. Henshaw replied.

At this point the man appeared and said that he wanted to go to Mount Huron.

Mrs. Henshaw answered for the social worker.

"You can't go because of your TB."

"But wouldn't you like to go to the Lakeview Sanatorium?" the social worker suggested. "Mrs. Henshaw and I have been talking it over."

"I guess it's the next best place," Mrs. Henshaw said.

While the conversation was far more devious and prolonged than these quotations indicate, this remark clinched the matter, and before the social worker left, Mr. Henshaw had signed the application for his admission to the sanatorium where ten days later he was comfortably established.

If in a situation of this sort one is known and liked by the individual in trouble there frequently comes the temptation to make a personal appeal to him: "Do this because I want it." Nothing is weaker, less constructive and less permanent. The contact between helper and helped usually is temporary. Remove the personality of the one who makes this plea and the reason for the course of conduct which he urges is likely also to disappear. This objection obviously does not hold where, as in the interview with the old gentleman described at the beginning of the chapter, the motive appealed to is that of making happy some one with whom there is a continuing relationship. The social worker was justified in emphasizing the wish of the old gentleman's niece that he move to more comfortable quarters. The tie between the two had always existed and would endure as long as life lasted. To please her would be a constant source of pleasure to himself, but for him to have acquiesced for no other reason than because he recognized the well-intentioned earnestness of the social worker would have been a scant guarantee of his holding to the plan that had been proposed. Personality, in the sense of the unconscious attraction which one human being exercises over another, must almost inevitably be a factor in motivation, but it should seldom, if ever, be deliberately used to influence decisions.

Often that which prevents people from entering institutions is the fear of the unknown. One way of overcoming such a difficulty is to suggest a visit to the hospital or the home in question. Seeing the place gives it a concreteness and definiteness that clears away the disturbing element of vagueness and uncertainty. Its inherent attractiveness both allays fear and provides an additional reason for seeking admission.

As a positive stimulus fear is one of the strongest of motives. It is responsible for many successful careers, careers that have found their genesis in the very fear that they would not be successful. The fear of what people might say, the fear of consequences has been a stabilizing force in countless lives and many a boy and girl brought up in country, village, or town has learned the beginnings of foresight and thrift through the haunting fear of the poorhouse.

Powerful though this motive is the use of it is the least desirable of all the ways of influencing individuals. Back of an appeal to it usually is the implication of force, and to apply force, as pointed out in Chapter X, is generally to confess a lack of skill and understanding. The use of all other motives partakes in greater or less degree of the nature of inspiration. To arouse fear is to command. The appeal to most motives leaves a man free to choose. It is a form of leadership. Fear drives.

Reward is a far sounder method of reinforcing an individual's desires. Lacking the same compulsory element, it can be used with greater justification. Obviously, opportunity for increased income is a more satisfactory way of developing a man's industrial efficiency than is the threat of the loss of his job. Interesting the individual in the task itself, work for the sake of work, would be still more constructive.

The influencing of a person through an appeal to his desires is seldom so clear cut and direct a process as the illustrations thus far would perhaps indicate. Actually, the shortest interview may involve calling upon such a variety of motives as to make it hard to classify them. While a knowledge and an understanding of the individual in need of help will usually indicate the appeal that may be most effective, one must frequently rely upon trial and error, stimulating this desire and that, until success is achieved. Often, as with the encouraging of the old gentleman to move to the suburbs, it is impossible to tell what motive has been decisive. Seldom is a man influenced by any one thing. Usually he is moved by a complexity of considerations. The part of the person who would help him is to make sure that all appropriate suggestions have been presented and that he has had the opportunity which the motives carry with them, an opportunity of the greatest

potentiality; for under the influence of a quick-
ened desire men have frequently accomplished —
are, indeed, constantly accomplishing — tasks to
which otherwise they would have never dreamed
themselves to be equal.

CHAPTER XIII

DYNAMICS

And the rain descended, and the floods came, and the winds blew, and beat upon that house; and it fell not: for it was founded upon a rock. (Matthew VII, 25.)

> She had an understanding with the years;
> For always in her eyes there was a light
> As though she kept a secret none might guess
> Some confidence that time had made her heart.
> So calmly did she bear the weight of pain,
> With such serenity accept the joy,
> It seemed she had a mother love for life,
> And all the days were children at her breast.
>
> SCUDDER MIDDLETON

POWERFUL though motivation is in stimulating men to action there are other forces that are even stronger. The marshalling of an individual's desires is in a sense a preliminary process. It starts him upon a given course of conduct. It is a means of focusing his initiative upon a specific and frequently an instant occasion, — helping him to decide to consult a physician, to enter an institution, to apply for a job, or to embark upon some other definite task. Usually its chief value is in its immediacy.

There are sources of strength that are more lasting, sources of power within the man himself and in the world about him, dynamics which are continually being used by people to raise the level of their energies and to cause them to flow surely and steadily through the channels into which they have been directed.

What is more familiar than such testimony as that of Mrs. Hearne who had been obliged to make the adjustment to widowhood under circumstances of peculiar difficulty.

"I could not have gone through with it," she said, "if it had not been for my faith."

Commonplace, also, are experiences like that of Herbert Worth, who, without family or kin to help him with affection and sympathy, found in his religion the courage to face the slow advance of cancer, or that of Wilson Kirk, who having given himself over to dissipation was converted at a gospel mission and completely reorganized his life, devoting the remainder of it to his church and to his family.

Here was a force that not only provided an initial impulse but also continued for many years to be a source of renewal and strength. In each of these persons it manifested itself differently but in all it was an inspiring and sustaining power.

Centuries of human experience have given

similar testimony to the dynamic qualities of religion. Again and again it is the decisive factor in enabling an individual to overcome his difficulties. Religion shows itself differently in different persons. To one it appears suddenly as in conversion; to another it comes as the growth of a slowly developing conviction. One man receives it through one form of faith, another through another form. This complicates the problem of using it, for the person who is in need of help may require an interpretation of religion different from that offered by the person who desires to help him. Yet so personal a thing is religion that one can express it only as he perceives it. He can give only his own interpretation of religion. This may, indeed, be the wisest thing to do. Often, however, it will happen that the man in trouble already has an approach to religion, one which perhaps may have been little used but which if developed might mean much to him. The best procedure with such a person is to bring him into touch with some one who has this same approach and who may be able to confirm him in it.

There is a valuable suggestion in the practice of social case workers in non-sectarian organizations. Their effort always is to strengthen whatever relationship may exist between a man and the institutionalized expression of the faith which he professes. While this practice is partially the result of a desire not to break denominational bounds it also rests upon the sound principle that in a time of distress an individual will be most likely to want to turn to the spiritual bases upon which in the past, even though remote, he may have begun to build.

This means more than merely telling a man that he ought to attend church or synagogue. It means bringing him into touch with some other human being, whether priest, social worker, or layman, who understands how best to interpret his faith in him.

This principle was put into ideal practice by the social case worker who opened the way to a more intimate relationship of a man with his church by helping him to move his family into a house next to one occupied by a devoted and active member of the same denomination. Telling him that he ought to go to church would have had little effect. It was through the life with his neighbor that he was brought to see the value of religion so that he once more attended services and experienced a quickening of his faith. The social worker who was instrumental in bringing this about subscribed to a creed that was different in many respects from that of her client, but she believed in the dynamic qualities of religion and therefore helped to strengthen him in those spiritual beliefs which seemed to make the greatest appeal to him. However religion expresses itself, it is the most vital thing in the life of the individual in whom it exists, the primary source of inspiration and anchorage, the influence that sustains and steadies him in every adjustment that he must make.

Wholly different in influence and character from religion was the dynamic utilized in arousing Margaret Seip, a woman of fifty, from the introspective state into which she had fallen. Miss Seip and her mother had been living together in two rooms with so little to do and such a barrenness of happenings that for lack of a better occupation they spent their days in telling each other about the miserable condition of their health. What they needed was a new subject for thought, something that would break the monotony with which they were surrounded. This was supplied when the daughter was placed at work in an arts and crafts shop. The comings and goings of the customers, the sight of new things, the conversation of the other employees gave the woman an excitement and an interest that she carried home with her at the end of the day for the vicarious enjoyment of her mother. "I didn't know people could talk about such cheerful things," she said in appreciation of what her work meant to her.

She had profited by what might be called the dynamic of adventure. Adventure, change, variety, new experience help to maintain an individual's alertness and to quicken his zest for living. It is frequently as much this as the physical advantage of climate that physicians have in mind when they prescribe the mountains or the seashore for a convalescing patient. It is what many people derive from travel. The woman who mastered a fit of depression by rearranging her furniture and giving a fresh aspect to her home was making excellent use of this dynamic of adventure and change.

Adventure has a contribution to make to the life of every human being. Depending as it does, however, upon variety and change it has not the substantial qualities of some of the other dynamics. It is a relish that usually needs to be accompanied or followed by meat. It was this sort of sequence that enabled Tony Patrello successfully to make the adjustment to adolescence. In the years that immediately succeeded his father's death he had been drifting farther and farther away from the influence of his home. At thirteen years of age he preferred the manners and habits of the street to those which his mother urged upon him. He was a frequent truant from school and a leader of a group of boys whose deviltries in the neighborhood threatened soon to bring them before the juvenile court. No appeal seemed to have any effect upon him.

One morning a social case worker happened to see Tony take his father's violin down from the wall. She asked him whether he would like to learn to play upon it. He thought that perhaps he would. Lessons at a neighboring settlement were arranged for immediately. It was a new experience and for nearly a month Tony was engrossed in it. He spent all his spare moments in practice and measured time by the intervals between his lessons. His attendance at school became regular, for the social worker had conditioned his instruction in music upon this, and he began to devote to his violin the leisure that had been wasted on the street. The dynamic of adventure possessed him and became the means of turning the stream of his energy into useful channels.

Then came a period when the newness wore off. Tony showed signs of slipping back to the old life. It now required all the ingenuity of the social worker to stimulate his desire to master the violin. Every conceivable motive was utilized until finally the boy reached the point of being able to make music, not by any means the music of a master but music that was appreciated as such by the other members of the family and of course by Tony, himself. The satisfaction that he derived from this accomplishment had a profound effect upon him. It took him altogether away from the street. His music began to develop in him new habits of behavior. It brought him new friends, and it strengthened the whole tone of his life. The sense of achievement he derived from being able to play upon the violin filled him with the ambition for achievement in other directions, and first in education and later in work he attained to one success after another. What the sense of adventure had begun the sense of achievement carried on.

Achievement is one of the most stimulating of life's experiences. The sense of power and of confidence which it brings strengthens one for further accomplishment. Look to the man who is listless or timorous or in despair and one is likely to find that he has nothing from which he can win for himself the feeling of success. And yet the opportunity for achievement is neither remote nor unusually difficult to find. It is often to be derived from the simplest and the homeliest things. To most bookkeepers there is no thrill like that which follows the striking of a balance at the first trial, unless it be that of eliminating the discrepant penny after hours of search. One woman enjoys a great sense of achievement as she looks at the garden she has just cleared of weeds. Another woman finds nothing that quite equals the satisfaction of a triple row of glasses of preserves, the product of a morning over the stove. One person obtains a sense of achievement from a piece of carpentry; another in polishing the household brass; a third in a well-played game of bridge. To reach the office and clear the desk of mail before the rest of the staff arrive is an exhilaration to many a business man who finds his whole day made more effective by this initial accomplishment. The sense of achievement may lie in the writing of a letter, or the making of a speech, or the vicarious success that is had through the accomplishment of a son or a daughter or a pupil. It may come in as many different ways as there are people. Always it is an influence for strength. Achievement begets achievement. The consciousness of success charges a man's energies to higher levels of effort and often what otherwise would have been impossible is attained.

While frequently the finding of the means by which an individual can derive a sense of achievement is a process of trial and error, involving the suggesting of this and then that until the appropriate medium has been discovered, it is obvious that the more intimately one knows a man the more likely will one be to select the thing that will attract him. Usually to learn what has given him a feeling of accomplishment in the past is to find what will satisfy him in his present difficulty.

A woman who was friendless, unhappy, and unstable consulted a social case worker. She had no pleasure in her work as seamstress. She was asked whether she had ever tried anything else. Yes, she had. She had been a cook, a lady's maid, a clerk in a store, and an operator in a factory. In none of these employments had she remained longer than a few months. Before her experience with them she had been a teacher of Spanish. For the first time during the conversation she showed enthusiasm. Evidently this was an occupation in which she had found self-expression. It developed that she had been an able teacher but that she was not the sort of person to work coöperatively with other people in an organization. She had been obliged to leave several schools and had thought that teaching was closed to her. The social worker found some private pupils for the woman. The experiment was successful. At the end of a year the teacher's clients had increased in number, and she was a more stable person than she had ever been.

Sometimes it is impossible, perhaps even unnecessary, to arrange for a change in an individual's employment. The task is rather to help him to see that what he is doing is important and that he is doing it well. Every craftsman no matter how sure he may be of his art is dependent upon the appraisal of his work by those whom he regards as competent critics. It is not unusual for a person to have a feeling of failure changed to one of achievement when what he thought to be unsuccessful is received with appreciation. The admiration which a social worker expressed for the needlework of a woman who felt that her education was wasted in this occupation was the means of giving her a new sense of accomplishment. To realize that some one whose opinion she respected recognized something unusual in her product and brought other people to see this also was enough to develop in her a much needed satisfaction and content.

Quite as influential as achievement in developing an individual's energies is the purposeful effort he makes in order to attain to success. Few things are more effective in enabling a man to overcome his difficulties. To have a goal toward which to work both quickens and steadies him. The winning of the great war was a means of re-creating for a time at least thousands of unhappy lives. For four years they had a cause so vital and so important that it gave new meaning to existence and new strength to being. The determination to obtain an education or to recover one's health or to pay one's debts or to build a business or to develop an invention or to accomplish any other ambition has a buoying and sustaining influence upon an individual's energies. If it is but one of a number of factors in his life and is not allowed to remain single in his mind and to occupy him to the exclusion of all else it can make him more vigorous in everything he does.

What the having of a purpose can accomplish for an individual is illustrated by the story of Mrs. Quinn.

Mrs. Quinn presented a paradox in that she loved her children and at the same time neglected them. For that matter she neglected herself. Neither their clothing nor hers was ever clean, and she allowed the house to become as unkempt as its tenants. She was an evasive person. It was easier for her to lie than to tell the truth, and she was rapidly teaching her children, both directly and by example, this method of approaching life. Yet she was gentle and affectionate with them and it was evident — at least to the social case worker — that any better ordering of Mrs. Quinn's life would come about through her devotion to the children.

Every attempt to use their welfare as a means of influencing her failed. Then came a crisis in Mrs. Quinn's affairs. One morning she called to see the social worker with the news that she had given up her home and had rented two furnished rooms to which she intended to move the family. The truth was that she had equipped the house in which she had been living by purchases from an installment company. She had failed in her payments, and the company had removed every piece of furniture from her home. Hitherto she had always insisted that the furniture was her own.

Mrs. Quinn had expected that the social worker would come to the rescue as she had on many another occasion. The social worker, however, saw in the woman's predicament an opportunity to help her to make a change in her way of life. Instead of offering the financial assistance that would have removed the immediate difficulty she agreed to the plan that Mrs. Quinn had suggested. Obviously, a family of seven ought not to live in two furnished rooms and it would be necessary to make provision elsewhere — either in an institution or in a private home — for at least three of the children. Mrs. Quinn was heart-broken. To be separated from her children was more than she could bear. She was told that there was a way by which she could reunite her family. All she need do was to demonstrate that she was a fit mother for them. Let her prove her ability to take proper care of the remaining children. Let her endeavor to train them to be truthful instead of setting them an opposite example, and the social worker would help her to reunite her household.

The change which took place in Mrs. Quinn was almost immediate. In two weeks her clothes and person were clean and she had made a beginning of furbishing her rooms. The habit of lying was not so easily broken, but she now attempted to meet life squarely. At the end of three months, the social worker felt that enough progress had been made to justify her in reëstablishing Mrs. Quinn in a house, but instead of returning all the children to her immediately, she arranged to have them restored, one at a time. Thus each child which Mrs. Quinn won back was an incentive to her to work the harder to make of herself the sort of mother she ought to be, and by the time the family was reunited, Mrs. Quinn had begun to prefer cleanliness for its own sake and to see that it was possible to be happy and still tell the truth.

Undoubtedly, the personality and influence of the social worker had much to do with this change, but what started it and gave it impetus was Mrs. Quinn's determination to win back her children. The real skill of the social worker lay in her perception that out of the crisis that had come into Mrs. Quinn's life a goal for her activities might be devised. There is no better place to look for the fabric of a purpose than at the very heart of an individual's difficulties.

What gave additional strength to the ordinary powers of this dynamic was its genesis in Mrs. Quinn's affection for her children. That she was devoted to them made her purpose to regain them the greater, while the struggle to bring them back to her increased her love for them. They were the principal medium through which her emotional life expressed itself.

Emotional expression when it has, as here, a satisfactory channel can be one of the most steadying and inspiring of influences. It finds its outlets variously, through appreciation of nature and of art, and through every phase of human association, acquaintanceship, friendship, courtship, marriage, parenthood, family life. It is in human association that it reaches its highest values, for here there is the element of response, the possibility of that reciprocity of affection that can bring security and satisfaction. Such emotional expression is not a thing to be sought. It is suspicious of invitations and it comes unbidden. It is a mutual experience, a harmony of free and understanding personalities.

One can introduce the lonely individual to

human association. One can take him where there are people who might become his friends, but unless he is clear of confining inhibitions and reservations his efforts at emotional expression will be fruitless and unsatisfying. While it is true that it is largely through emotional expression that personality finds its release, nevertheless, a measure of preparation for this experience is possible. Certainly this applied to the solution of Lydia Easton's difficulties.

Lydia had had an unsettled and an unsatisfactory childhood. Her father had died when she was a baby and her mother had moved about from place to place selling books and leaving her children to form what associates they could in her absence. It was a haphazard sort of life and the girl had always looked forward to the time when in a family of her own she might have that which hitherto she had lacked. Her desire for affection laid her open to seduction and she had scarcely reached twenty years of age when a baby was born to her whose father's previous marriage prevented him from becoming her husband. She left her mother and sisters taking the child with her.

She now began wearing a wedding ring and spoke of herself as a widow. She almost succeeded in convincing herself of the truth of her story. When, before two years had passed, she was about to be confined again, this time having become involved with another man, she insisted that she had been assaulted.

She gave the social case worker a most circumstantial account of her marriage and even went with her to call upon the clergyman who she said had performed the ceremony. She was willing to prosecute the man whom she accused of being the father of her second child, although she had been intimate with several other men.

The motive underlying all this was her desire for a normal family life. Rather than be wholly without it she preferred to imagine it. Thereby she was, of course, making impossible the attainment of the very thing she wanted. Realizing this the social worker tried to help the girl to face the facts of her situation so that she might ultimately free herself for the forming of a wholesome married life. The visit to the clergyman was only one of the measures taken to convince the young woman that she was not married and that it would be wiser for her to recognize this. When even the clergyman's denial of the ceremony did not cause her to face the facts, the social worker

used for this purpose the prosecution of the father
of the second child, the woman having entered
suit upon the uninformed advice of a neighbor.
The case might have been dropped but the social
worker saw in it the one chance of clearing the un-
realities from the girl's life. Nor until the young
woman had admitted the truth on the witness
stand did she appreciate the extent to which she
had been living on a false basis and begin to face
life squarely. An opportunity now offered itself
for her to make her home with a family. Here as a
mother's helper she spent a year that was happier
than any other previous year in her history, the
only shadow upon it being the death of her first
child. She was made to feel that she had a genuine
share in the family life, the nearest approach to a
home that she had experienced. Then she met a
man whose earlier career had been as unhappy as
her own. In the marriage which followed she
found the true realization of her desires, incident-
ally after the birth of their first child reëstablishing for her husband ties with his own relatives
which had long been broken.

Undoubtedly it was in the having of a family of
her own that the solution of the young woman's
problem lay. In helping her to clear her life of un-

reality the social worker prepared her for the happiness that she later experienced. And is one not justified even in a situation of this sort in taking into consideration the possibility of marriage? After all most people marry and it is in the family that the emotional values of life can find complete expression; for here they are all mingled — the love of man and woman, the being together, the sharing of experiences, the sense of personal relationship with tradition, of oneness with past generations; the satisfaction of the longing to belong somewhere, to have a place in the world, to have a refuge from storm, to feel the security of mutual confidence, of being emancipated from impersonality and of being personal, of being utterly and completely one's self and of being thus beloved.

Family life includes the whole cycle from childhood to parenthood, but there is opportunity for renewal and strength in its every phase. Even to approximate it, as two women in their late thirties did in establishing a home of their own and adopting two children, is to find a sure vehicle for emotional expression. That is why there runs through nearly every one of the personal histories that have appeared in these chapters the effort to safeguard and develop family life. Let a man have a happy family relationship and the making of all his adjustments is facilitated.

Where this is not possible the use of every other available dynamic becomes of supreme importance. Emotional expression through other channels — through friendship, through the appreciation and enjoyment of nature, and through the cultivation of any latent artistic abilities — should be encouraged. There should be a search for new goals, for new purposes. More mediums for the sense of achievement should be secured. The spiritual life of men becomes, if possible, of even greater importance. Just as the person who is blind develops a compensating alertness in his other senses, so must the individual who is blocked from one dynamic be helped to a larger and more varied use of the rest.

But to contemplate the absence of any dynamic is as difficult as to conceive the loss of any of the senses. All are essential. All must be cultivated. The more and the broader a man's contacts with them the stronger and the fuller will flow the stream of his energies. They are the very essence of life. Let him possess them and the mastery of the art of living will be his.

CHAPTER XIV

IN CONCLUSION

What a piece of work is a man! how noble in reason! how infinite in faculty! in form and moving how express and admirable! in action how like an angel! in apprehension how like a god! the beauty of the world! the paragon of animals! (*Hamlet*, Act II, Scene 2.)

THERE can be no conclusion to a discussion of the art of helping any more than there can be a last chapter in the art of living; for living continues as long as life, and life touches life subtly and unmeasurably down through the generations. Forever, while man is part of the universe, the process of adjustment will endure, always involving new relationships and new situations, shaping and changing him and carrying with it ever the issue of happiness or trouble.

Each one of us, limited though his days may be, is caught up in the sweep of this vast ebb and flow of life. Nature working within him expresses herself in terms of her own timelessness. She is unhurried. Growth is a product of the years. Man, being but part of the whole, may become impatient, content with what would be incomplete. Nature is comprehensive and eternal.

To have grasped this lesson is to have made a beginning of learning the art of helping. We are continually seeking the immediate. We search for panaceas and we want instantaneous change. In a few days we would make different a human being who for three or four decades has been evolving to what he is. Yet if the body develops so slowly that in age one can recognize the youth, how can we expect greater rapidity in the transformation of personality which must express itself through the body and which is influenced by it.

Unfortunately, our very books contribute to the illusion that change in man is an easy and an expeditious process. When in three or four hundred pages the biography of a lifetime may be reviewed, the years themselves seem to take on a kind of cinematographic speed and unconsciously we come to expect the same instantaneous development in the people about us. The illustrations that have been used in the preceding pages may each have required a very few moments for the reading, but they represent for the most part months and years of effort. Moreover, these stories are cross-sections. They are not the whole life. The necessity of describing the application of a principle has placed an emphasis upon one incident to the exclusion of many other important occurrences.

Nor can it be said that after one, two, or three years an individual has achieved a permanent adjustment. There is no such thing as permanency in adjustment, for adjustment is constant change. Always a new crisis is arising, a new event occurring; and the whole struggle must be gone over with again. Not until the whole of a man's career is reviewed can a verdict be announced. While life is being lived, one can only say that thus far the individual has succeeded in overcoming his difficulties and in building wisely for the future.

In some situations a successful adjustment is not possible. There are wildernesses of the mind from which to the eye of present knowledge there seems to be no egress. This applies not merely to the person who is feeble-minded or who is suffering from some chronic form of mental disease, but also to the large number of people who live in that psychic borderland which divides the clearly normal and usual from the clearly abnormal and unusual, the people of whom science admits its ignorance by such diagnoses as constitutionally inferior, psycho-neurotic, and the like. For these unhappy individuals any but the most temporary adjustment is exceedingly difficult. They seem to be unable to hold long to any one course and they sink before the slightest waves of circumstance. With such persons, and with many others, our very ignorance often renders us incapable of helping where help is needed. Just as before the discovery of the antitoxins for diphtheria and tetanus hundreds of people died whose lives might have been prolonged, so, for the lack of knowledge of many things we are unable to aid individuals in the making of adjustments that in the future may be facilitated through the development of new techniques. There are limitations, also, of physique and environment which prevent the person in trouble from achieving anything but a life that, judged by the standards of persons of greater opportunity and endowment, would at best be unsatisfactory. There are great handicaps in the absence of the institutions which in time our municipalities and states will establish. It may be evident that the only solution of a man's difficulties lies in a stay in a psychopathic hospital, but if there is no room for him he must forego treatment. The same issue arises in dealing with feeble-mindedness, in the treatment of tuberculosis, and in many other problems. Small wonder is it that often when success in helping a human being might be expected it is failure that is met with instead.

On the other hand, the changes that take place in people are greater than we realize. In our search for the dramatic we overlook the very strength of nature's workmanship. We expect a revolution and fail to see the far more certain, though more gradual, process of evolution. When we realize the handicaps under which the greater part of humanity labors; when we consider the close physical proximity in which most people live with one another, and the ignorance, and the malnutrition, and the lack of recreation, and the years spent in an unfavorable environment; the accomplishments of the weakest and poorest individual become colossal. It must never be forgotten that with life as it is to-day the greatest material achievement that most men can hope for is the bare support of a family on the margin of existence. It is only the person who is situated in especially fortunate circumstances, or who has very unusual combinations of native endowment and character, who can win the means of obtaining the cultural and æsthetic opportunities that add much of beauty and interest to life. The vast majority of people live their lives through without even securing for their homes the kind of dwelling that would give them the environment they desire — no matter how modest their wants in this direction may be. Yet, in spite of these and many other handicaps, men attain to happiness, attain to it out of the barest of equipments and with the least of facilities.

No one who has watched the making of such an adjustment as the adjustment to tuberculosis, can fail to wonder at the marvels of which the average human being is capable. To realize the eternal watchfulness that is the means by which the consumptive wins the mastery of his life; to sense the steadfastness of purpose, the control of self, and the persistence which the living of a regularized existence involves; to appreciate what the foregoing of physical recreation and the limitation to his hours of activity mean; to realize all this and then to see men find contentment in spite of their disease, is to know that man can adjust himself to anything.

The more one works with people in trouble, the greater his confidence in human kind and his respect for human beings becomes. Seeing what they accomplish in overcoming their difficulties brings an ever deepening faith in their capacity for self-help. Let a man be free to be himself and his success is almost assured. Aid him, if he asks it, to a realization of the adjustment which he must make, interpreting to him, if need be, those with whom he is associated. Quicken his desires, if quickening they require, or show him that from which he can derive stability and inspiration. Encourage him to make his own plans, and to do his own thinking, and through it all strive to see him as he is and to understand and appreciate him.

This is the point of view from which social case workers approach the difficulties of the men and the women who come to them for help. It is a point of view to be sought by every person who is so placed that he may influence other people. It is as applicable in the daily relationships of life as it is in the most complicated forms of trouble. It is a philosophy that any one may apply to the making of his own adjustments.

To him who thus strives to understand his fellows and their problems life begins to reveal itself in deepening richness and wonder. The old fears, the old prejudices disappear leaving him free to perceive the truth, the truth whose facets are myriad so that one may gaze upon it through eternity and not make an ending. Out of life's very difficulties, out of our own frailty comes renewed appreciation of all that living can mean and the privilege that is ours in its practice. Who does not thrill at the miracle of being alive and of holding comradeship with that most marvelous of creatures, his fellow man! Transcending the vicissitudes of experience is the challenge of the greatest of the arts.

THE END